Marriage Bonds
and
Ministers' Returns
of
Chesterfield County, Virginia

1771-1815

Compiled By:
Catherine Lindsay Knorr

Southern Historical Press, Inc.
Greenville, South Carolina

SOUTHERN HISTORICAL PRESS, INC.
PO BOX 1267
Greenville, SC   29601

ISBN #0-89308-250-3

Printed in the United States of America

To

Mr. John Frederick Dorman III

Washington, D. C.

("The Virginia Genealogist")

and

Mr. William Perry Johnson

Raleigh, North Carolina

("The North Carolinian")

who are

two young men after my own heart.

Henrico
1634

Goochland
1726

CHESTERFIELD
1749

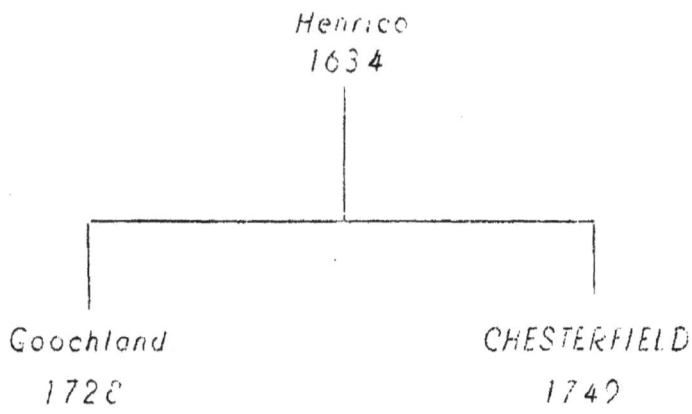

(Robinson: Chart 5, Page 160)

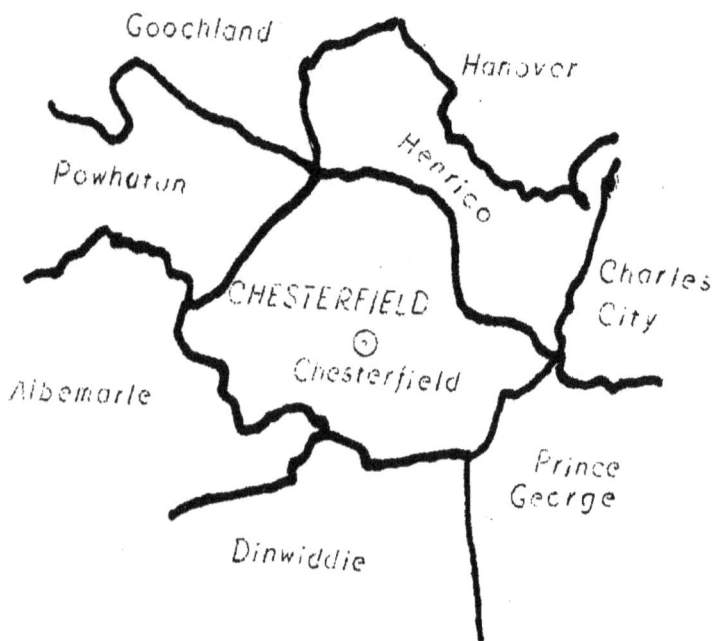

Goochland

Hanover

Powhatan

Henrico

Charles
City

CHESTERFIELD

⊙
Chesterfield

Albemarle

Prince
George

Dinwiddie

In their eager pursuit of ancestors, thousands of persons, far and near, whose roots go deep into a dozen Virginia counties, have discovered gratefully that Catherine Lindsay Knorr's compilations of marriage bonds and minister's returns have been a key asset to their search. To the list of localities covered previously in her patient, diligent research, she now for the first time assembles in this volume the scattered marital records of Chesterfield, whose history ante-dates that of Jamestown itself.

We are fortunate that a worker with Mrs. Knorr's genealogical background should have sacrificed so much of her leisure, and money too, poring over the tedious, and not always accurate old script, whose quaint orthography leads to the conclusion that the penman frequently was spelling by ear and writing with an over worked quill. To do this with her thoroughness, one must not only know where to look, but must be conversant fully with names of individuals and families and to have the rare ability to translate the fading, blurred and seemingly indecipherable writing.

In this study of one period in Chesterfield's past, Mrs. Knorr fills one of the numerous gaps in that ancient area's remarkable, but poorly documented history. Visited by Captain Christopher Newport in a search for a site for a settlement, Chesterfield was his avowed choice, but unfortunately he was over-ruled and thus the less favorable Jamestown Island won its niche in New World history. In the years that followed, Chesterfield has not been given recognition always for the accomplishments of its men and women because the first 140 years of its occupancy by the white race the county simply was a part of a vast region known as Henrico and its legal, military, church and social life was secondary and thus its identity as a locality naturally was submerged. Even after it became a separate political entity in 1749 this condition continued to a large extent because of its borders, north and south, there sprung the two natural trading posts from which came Richmond and Petersburg and these well publicized cities have managed to get credit for much of the diversified and eventful career of the more modest Chesterfield.

Yet, in the proper Chamber of Commerce spirit, Chesterfield may well call itself Virginia's "county of firsts". Within its borders iron ore was dug in 1608 and in 1619 America's first iron furnace was established. Nearby the first lead was found and in 1709 the first American coal was mined. Bermuda Hundred was the nation's first incorporated town and there the first will devising land was written in 1617 and probated four years later.

i

America's first recorded hospital was established as early as 1611 at Dutch Gap. As part of Henrico, Chesterfield would have shared the site of the nation's first University - Henricopolis - which was wiped out in 1622 by the greatest of the India massacres that afflicted the new Colony. Chesterfield did gain one school "first" with the establishment at Cobb's of an institution for the education of deaf-mutes and another during the Civil War when the Confederacy's only official educational project, the Naval Academy, was either aboard ship in Chesterfield waters or in huts within the Drewry's Bluff fortifications.

In the Bermuda Hundred section John Rolfe first cultivated tobacco scientifically; higher up in the county was Virginia's first "artificial" or paved road and nearby Bosher's Dam was the state's first multi-purpose dam, built for navigation as well as for water storage and power.

The state's first tramway, and second in the nation, was in Chesterfield and in 1829 Virginia's first railroad was put in operation wholly within the county. In the county was the first mill to manufacture the salt-peter so vitally needed during the Revolution.

Oddly, North America's largest diamond was found in Chesterfield and for many years the county was the nation's largest producer of ochre. The county furnished Virginia's first notary public - St. George Tucker - and in modern times it was the state's pioneer in the establishment of the trial justice court and was the first county to have a full-time sanitation officer and visiting nurse. Chesterfield even was the birthplace of the nationally observed Father's Day.

While these important events were taking place, Chesterfield suffered from many things of another nature. It rose twice from horrible Indian depredations; it suffered many tragic mine disasters and floods. During the Revolution it was ravashe by Redcoats and in the Civil War its soil again was drenched wit blood.

The war depredations removed forever many documents vital to Chesterfield's history, but time, neglect and carelessness, also conspire to make the work of the researcher difficult and the complete absence of early Chesterfield parish records, including the vestry books. Not a single one, prior to the Revolution, is known to exist. For many years Chesterfield was a part of the Henrico and Bristol Parishes, but such of their records that have been preserved are incomplete and unhappily the gaps missing usually are the ones of interest to the county. Not onl have the Chesterfield Colonial parish records vanished, but all

Episcopal edifices likewise are gone and in many instances even the sites are not known positively.

Court records likewise have suffered from various causes. The first county court house was burned in 1781 by General William Phillips while Benedict Arnold ravished the more populated areas where the churches, such as they were, stood directly in the path of the invader. When the court house was burned many of the valuable files were saved through the devotion of Clerk Benjamin Watkins, but even his valiant efforts could not rescue them all. Again in the Civil War, Clerk Nathan Cogbill carted important records to a place of safety, but it was inevitable that numerous documents were lost or destroyed. Arnold, again in 1781, made off with vital Henrico records which tied in with early Chesterfield.

Because of their quasi-official status, parishes of the Established Church in most instances are especially valuable to the geneological researcher. But here again Chesterfield is in the unhappy position of having absolutely none to turn to for the period prior to the Revolution. From the earliest days of the Colony until 1641-43, when Bristol Parish was authorized, Chesterfield was entirely within Henrico Parish. The few widely scattered plantations and settlements in what is now Chesterfield were served as early as 1611 by a church at Henricopolis on a peninsula, now an island, in the James River, with the rector, the Rev. Alexander Whitaker, having his residence and glebe lands at Coxendale, on the Chesterfield side of the stream. The church at Henricopolis was not salvaged from the desolation of the massacre of 1622 and a site safer from a surprise attack by the savages was substituted at a point lower down the river and on its north side where it continued to serve the adjacent Chesterfield area.

When Bristol Parish, on both sides of the Appomattox River, was established the "mother" church was at Bermuda Hundred. After 1700 the northwest section of what is now Chesterfield received an influx of French refugees, the Huguonots, and that area became a part of Prince William Parish.

The Curl's Church, near Varina, in Henrico, continued to serve the upper James River section of Chesterfield, but over strong protests on account of the inconvenience, although those parishoners above Falling Creek now could cross the river to a small adjunct of the Henrico Parish church on Chapel Island, now the foot of Richmond's Eighteenth Street, and later they went up the steep hills to worship in the new St. John's where Patrick Henry later sounded his clarion call for liberty. St. John's dates from 1741 and its fragramentary vestry records have numerous names that may be identified with the Chesterfield area.

iii

Meanwhile Bristol Parish was extending its coverage of the present Chesterfield area and in 1723 the vestry book records a contract to Thomas Jefferson, grandfather of the future President for the erection of a brick structure variously called Old Church, Jefferson's Church and Ware's Bottom Church. The build stood adjacent to the Hopewell-Richmond road (Route 10) about on mile from Route 1. It probably became the new "mother" church of Bristol Parish, but here again is another of those exasperating gaps.

Bristol Parish, on the opposite side of the Appomattax, was outgrowing the parent segment and there came a separation in 1735 when Chesterfield was granted its own exclusive parish which was appropriately named Dale in honor of the far-sighted English man who had established the towns of Henricopolis and Bermuda Hundred and was a devout, even fanatical, churchman. The first rector of Dale Parish was the Rev. Zachariah Brooke. Jefferson Church evidently became the seat of the parish activities. Nothing remains of this edifice, while the two only surviving gravestones in the adjacent cemetery bear the dates 1772 and 17

The established Church in Chesterfield, as well as in othe sections of the Old Dominion, was falling into disrepute many years before the Revolution, although Archibald Cary, of Ampthi was a militant supporter who did not hesitate to bring many dis senters into court. Among these was a group of itinerant preac ers of a Baptist sect who were thrown in jail, not for preachin the gospel as most people claim, but because they failed, and in some instances, refused to secure the required and available license to preach.

The activities of these itinerant preachers adds another barrier to the compilation of complete marital records. Not being licensed they performed marriages without the requisite preliminaries and then in many instances they neglected to repo their illegal service. Sometimes belated returns were made, often confusing the marriage dates.

Sir William Gooch, the Royal governor of Virginia, signed the "Commission of the Peace" which officially created Chester-field County. It was dated May 12, 1749 and was addressed to William Kennon, John Bolling, William Gay, Richard Royall, William Kennon, Jr., John Archer, Richard Eppes, Seth Ward, John Royall, William Eppes, Robert Goode, Henry Randolph, Edward Osborne, Jr., and Richard Kennon.

The first clerk was Benjamin Watkins. John Archer became the first sheriff with Grief Randolph as undersheriff. The surveyor was George Currie and Augustine Claiborne was Chesterfield's first deputy King's Counsel.

Under the Commission the first session of the Chesterfield Court was "holden" on June 2, 1749, when the newly designated justices took the oath of office. The new county was represented in the House of Burgesses for the first time on February 5, 1752. John Bolling, a former Henrico burgess, and Richard Eppes were its first representatives. Williamsburg was now the capital.

Chesterfield's "Commission of the Peace" was one of the country's long missing documents. In 1953, while Chesterfield, An Old Virginia County was about to go to press, it was my good fortune to acquire the document which had been "removed" from the court house by a Federal soldier and in some way had come into the hands of a book dealer in upper New York after having been in an institution for many years. Suitably framed, it now hangs in the county court house.

As an indication of the difficulty with names in early documents, two justices were named properly twice in the body of the Commission as Richard Royall and John Royall, yet on the reverse side the name is spelled Royal by the clerk, apparently immediately after the first court session. Osborne and Eppes are among other familiar Chesterfield names variously spelled.

Mrs. Knorr's primary source of information was the Marriage Register compiled by the Virginia State Library a number of years ago from the loose bonds that were gradually disappearing. She received additional data from the Rev. William Cameron's register while he was rector of Bristol Parish. Ministerial returns, where there were also bonds, were copied by Mrs. Knorr with a proper notation, often with the name of the church in which the ceremony was performed. Where there was no bond, she infers that the bride lived in Chesterfield, but the groom elsewhere.

Obviously had court records been more complete and had parish papers been available for research, Mrs. Knorr could have thrown interesting light on earlier Chesterfield marriages. Her starting date was at the beginning of a period of great uncertainty. Methodist and Baptist congregations, neither of which kept reliable records, were just beginning to get organized and even the new Manchester Parish, which had just come into being, soon withered. Its records vanished long since and the site of its church is vaguely described as "twelve miles southwest" of Richmond.

While the period covered by Mrs. Knorr is from 1771 through 1815, it is remarkable that she lists 1770 marriages and her in-

dex will prove a great time saver for the inexperienced researcher. I salute her for this contribution to Virginiana.

Francis Early Lutz

Richmond, Virginia
1 November 1958

****

Books by Mrs. Knorr

Marriage Bonds and Ministers' Returns of Prince Edward Co.
Virginia, 1754-1810 (1950)

Marriage Bonds and Ministers' Returns of Charlotte Co., Virginia
1764-1815 (1951)

Marriage Bonds and Ministers' Returns of Sussex Co., Virginia
1754-1810 (1951)

Marriage Bonds and Ministers' Returns of Brunswick Co., Virginia
1750-1810 (1953)

Marriage Bonds and Ministers' Returns of Fredericksburg, Virginia
1782-1850 (1954)

Marriages of Culpeper County, Virginia 1781-1815 (1954)

Marriage Bonds and Ministers' Returns of Greensville Co, Virginia
1781-1825 (1955)

Marriage Bonds and Ministers' Returns of Southampton Co., Virginia
1750-1810 (1955)

Marriage Bonds and Ministers' Returns of Pittsylvania Co.,
Virginia 1767-1805 (1956)

Marriage Bonds and Ministers' Returns of Powhatan County, Virginia
1777-1830 (1957)

Marriage Bonds and Ministers' Returns of Halifax Co., Virginia
1753-1800 (1957)

Marriage Bonds and Ministers' Returns of Chesterfield Co.,
Virginia 1771-1815 (1958)

Mrs. H. A. Knorr
1401 Linden Street
Pine Bluff, Arkansas

_____ 1792. _____ and Martha Cousins. Married by Rev. Eleazer Clay, Baptist. Manuscript mutilated. Ministers' Returns p. 380.

_____ 1792. _____ and Sarah Moore. Married by Rev. Eleazer Clay, Baptist. Manuscript mutilated. Ministers Returns p. 380.

_____ 1792. _____ and Fanney Morrisete. Married by Rev. Eleazer Clay, Baptist. Manuscript mutilated. Ministers' Returns p. 380.

_____ 1792. _____ and Martha Newby. Married by Rev. Eleazer Clay, Baptist. Manuscript mutilated. Ministers' Returns p. 380.

17 December 1802. Thomas ABBE and Jincy _____. Married by Rev. Henry Featherstone, Sr. Ministers' Returns p. 396.

23 January 1790. Thomas ADAMS and Sally Morrison. Robert Goude (Goode) guardian of Sally consents for her. No relationship stated. This is consent only. p. 30.

4 March 1787. William ADAMS and Elizabeth Landrum. Sur. William Howard. p. 25.

25 January 1800. John ADDISON and Elizabeth Graves. Sur. John McKim. Wit. Elizabeth McKim. p. 59.

22 February 1790. Joshua ADKERSON and Frances Haskins, dau. of Robert Haskins who consents. This is consent only. Married by Rev. John Goode. p. 30.

8 October 1803. Burwell ADKINS and Elizabeth Fowler or Towler. Sur. Mark Farmer. p. 69.

5 May 1804. George ADKINS and Frances Bottom. Sur. Reuben Bottom. This marriage is in a list returned by Rev. Henry Bridgewater dated 6 May 1814. p. 72.

8 April 1805. George ADKINS and Elizabeth Woodcock. 21 years of age, dau. of Robert Woodcock. Sur. Henry Woodcock. Married by Rev. Charles Hopkins. Returned 11 May 1805. p. 76.

13 January 1805. James ADKINS and Lucy Morgan, dau. of John Morgan, deceased. John J. Kleinhoff guardian of Lucy consents for her. Sur. Ambrose Alexander. p. 80.

1

19 December 1793. John ADKINS and Polley Franklin. Married by
Rev. Thomas Hardie, Methodist. Ministers Returns p. 381.

14 December 1799. Joseph ADKINS and Tabitha Chalkley. Married
by Rev. Thomas Hardie, Methodist. Ministers' Returns p. 389.

10 April 1809. William ADKINS and Mary Moseley Skelton, dau. o
Isaac Skelton who consents and is surety. p. 97.

15 December 1808. Arthur AIKIN and Ann Beasley, widow of Thoma
Beasley. Sur. Elam Lockett. p. 94.

12 March 1782. James AIKEN and Sally Pleasant. Sur. William
Aiken. p. 16.

19 October 1783. Jo AIKEN and ___ _____. Omitted from p. 19.
p. 57.

13 July 1786. Arthur AKIN and Elizabeth Pleasant. Married by
Rev. John Goode. Ministers' Returns p. 371.

13 September 1797. Arthur AKIN and Mary Cheatham. Married by
Rev. Needler Robinson, Rector Dale Parish Episcopal Church.
Ministers' Returns p. 390.

June 1786-June 1787. James AKIN and Elizabeth Hancock. Marrie
by Rev. Eleazer Clay, Baptist. Ministers Returns p. 372.

18 September 1805. James AKIN and Judith Baker, dau. of Willia
Baker who consents. Sur. Robert Brummale. James Akin 21 years
of age. Married 19 September by Rev. Thomas Lafon, Church of
Christ. p. 78.

9 September 1789. John AKIN and Mary Lockett. Sur. Isham
Cheatham. p. 28.

7 October 1806. Robert AKIN and Lavinia G. Clay, dau. of Eleaz
Clay who consents. Sur. Matthew Clay. Married 8 October by Re
Thomas Lafon, Church of Christ. p. 83.

_____ _____ 1790. John AKINS and Mary Lockett. Married by Rev
John Goode. Return dated 6 April 1790. Ministers' Returns
p. 376.

20 June 1796. Reuben ALLEN and Mary Edwards. Married by Rev.
Thomas Hardie, Methodist. Ministers' Returns p. 383.

9 March 1807. Robert ALLEN and Elizabeth Brechan, dau. of Jusia Brechan. Sur. John Rozel. Wit. Thomas Turner. p. 86.

25 August 1786. Samuel ALLEN and Linchy Lockett. Sur. Edward Branch. p. 24.

8 August 1814. Jacob ALPIN and Martha Gates, dau. of Joseph Gates who consents. Sur. Henry Bowman. Wit. Beverly Chew Stanard. Married 13 August by Rev. John Wooldridge of Powhatan County. p. 125.

9 March 1809. James ALVIS and Peggy Watkins, widow of John Watkins. Sur. Edward Burnett. Wit. Suzanna Haskins. p. 96.

11 January 1811. Zephaniah ALVIS and Lucy Horner, dau. of Abijah Horner who consents. Sur. Owen Franklin. Wit. Edward Burnett. Married 12 January by Rev. Jordan Martin. p. 106.

30 January 1798. Charles AMMONETT and Phebe Hall. Sur. Aaron Lyra. Wit. T. Watkins. Married 1 February by Rev. Benjamin Watkins. p. 50.

14 April 1794. James AMMONETT and Mary Short, dau. of John Short who consents. Sur. James Stanford. Married by Rev. James Smith of Powhatan County. p. 38.

5 December 1789. Henry ANDERSON and Elizabeth Bass. Married by Rev. Needler Robinson, Rector Dale Parish, Episcopal Church. Ministers' Returns p. 374.

24 May 1805. Joel ANDERSON and Polley Johnson, dau. of David Johnson. Sur. Littleberry Andrews. Wit. William P. Dyer. p. 76.

14 February 1799. John ANDERSON and Fanny Moore. Sur. Vaden Gill. Wit. Thomas Finney. Married 16 February by Rev. Thomas Hardie, Methodist. p. 55.

8 January 1800. John ANDERSON and Elizabeth Smith, dau. of Marvin Smith who consents. Wit. Joseph Roper and Drury Roper. This is consent only. Married 11 January by Rev. Benjamin Watkins. p. 59.

7 September 1772. Matthew ANDERSON and Judith Branch, dau. of Olive Branch (father) who consents and is surety. Marriage register says this bond was omitted from page 1. p. 13.

10 April 1785. Nathan ANDERSON and Maryan Mayo. Sur. Thomas Bass, Sr. p. 22.

31 March 1790. Ralph C. ANDERSON and Mary Wilkinson, dau. of William Wilkinson who consents. This is consent only. Married by Rev. John Goode. p. 30.

13 August 1794. Robert ANDERSON and Sally Clark Smith, dau. of Mourning Smith (mother) who consents. Wit. Jeremiah Mole. This is consent only. Married by Rev. James Smith. p. 39.

9 April 1811. Spencer B. ANDERSON and Nancy Traylor, dau. of William Traylor who consents and is surety. Married 17 April by Rev. Joseph Gill. p. 108.

27 October 1797. William ANDERSON and Avis Rudd, dau. of Elizabeth Rudd who consents. Sur. Archibald Beasley. Wit. T. Watkins and Thomas Finney. Married 28 October by Rev. James Rucks. p. 48.

22 August 1812. William ANDERSON and Rebecca M. Anderson. Sur Thomas Anderson. Wit. Edward W. Anderson. p. 115.

18 December 1813. Benjamin ANDREWS and Michey (or Magee) Marsh dau. of Aaron and Sarah Marsh who consent. Sur. Walthall Marsh Wit. Elizabeth Andrews and Sarah Marsh. See Simon Andrews. p. 123.

31 January 1814. Erasmus ANDREWS and Lockey Blankenship, 21 years of age. Dau. of Beverly Blankenship, deceased, and Jane Blankenship who consents. Sur. Wilson H. Vaden. Married 3 February by Rev. Thomas Lafon, Church of Christ. p. 123.

8 December 1785. Isham ANDREWS and Mary Purkinson, dau. of Baxter Purkinson who consents. Married 3 Feb. 1786 by Rev. William Leigh, Rector Manchester Parish, Episcopal Church who says Perkinson. p. 23.

4 February 1812. Jacob ANDREWS and Nancy Dyer, both 21 years of age. Sur. John Belcher. Married 5 February by Rev. Joseph Gill. p. 112.

10 December 1812. John H. ANDREWS and Polley W. Dance, dau. of Ezekiel Dance who consents and is surety. p. 117.

24 January 1815. John ANDREWS and Patience Smith, 23 years old 6 day next June, dau. of Charles Smith, deceased, and Mary Smith. Sur. David Franklin. Married 26 January by Rev. Joseph Gill, Jr. p. 128.

29 March 1802. Mark ANDREWS and Lezi Stiles, dau. of Sarah Stiles who consents. Wit. William Stiles. p. 65.

12 May 1806. Randolph ANDREWS and Agness Moore. Sur. Aaron Marsh. p. 81.

23 December 1813. Simon ANDREWS and Mickey Marsh. Married by Rev. Joseph Gill, Jr. See Benjamin Andrews. Ministers' Returns p. 408.

7 January 1802. William ANDREWS and Pheby Dyer. Married by Rev. Thomas Hardie, Methodist. Ministers' Returns p. 395.

21 December 1805. Bevill ARCHER and Nancy Perdue, 21 years of age, dau. of Ezekiel Perdue, deceased. Sur. John Perdue. p. 80.

10 April 1797. Edward ARCHER and Mary Jefferson Bolling, dau. of John Bolling who consents. Sur. Robert Bolling. Wit. Archibald Bolling, Jr. Married 27 May by Rev. Needler Robinson, Rector Dale Parish, Episcopal Church. p. 47.

29 August 1799. Edward ARCHER and Ann Walthall. Married by Rev. Needler Robinson, Rector Dale Parish, Episcopal Church. Ministers' Returns p. 390.

10 February 1794. Field ARCHER and Martha Bolling, dau. of John Bolling who consents. Wit. Rebecca Thornton. This is consent only. Married 20 February by Rev. Needler Robinson. Rector Dale Parish, Episcopal Church. p. 38.

25 November 1803. Field ARCHER and Eliza Stils. Married by Rev. Henry Featherstone, Sr. Ministers' Returns p. 396.

_____ 1792. John ARCHER and Mary Blankenship. Married by Rev. Eleazer Clay, Baptist. Ministers' Returns p. 380.

30 July 1795. John H. ARCHER and Clarissa Noble. Sur. Daniel Totty. Wit. William Finney. Name also given John Archer. Married by Rev. Needler Robinson, Rector Dale Parish, Episcopal Church who says John Archer. Returned 27 August. p. 41.

1 June 1808. John ARCHER and Elizabeth Chamberlayne Batte. Sur. John Stratton. p. 91.

13 September 1813. John H. ARCHER and Rebecca Wilkinson Baugh, 21 years of age. Sur. Creed Berry. Married 16 September by Rev. Joseph Gill, Jr. p. 122.

23 January 1787. Peterfield ARCHER and Elizabeth Walthall. Archibald Walthall guardian of Elizabeth consents for her. This is consent only. p. 25.

5

11 September 1809. Dr. Robert P. ARCHER and Frances Walthall,
dau. of Archibald Walthall, deceased. Sur. Charles Ed(ward)
Featherstone. Wit. Edward Archer. p. 98.

28 December 1795. Stephen ARCHER and Fanney Patrum. Married by
Rev. Nathan Anderson, Methodist. Ministers' Returns p. 383.

8 February 1796. William ARCHER and Unity Claiborne Jones. Wit
John Friend. Unity signs her own consent. This is consent only
Married 25 February by Rev. Needler Robinson, Rector Dale Parish
Episcopal Church. p. 43.

21 December 1804. Henry ARCHIBALD and Elizabeth Sallee', widow
of John Sallee'. Sur. Benjamin Smith. Wit. Elizabeth Moody.
Married 22 December by Rev. Benjamin Watkins. p. 75.

_____ _____ 1791. Daniel ASHBROOK and Phebe Gates. Married by
Rev. Walthall Robertson, Baptist. Return dated 14 November 1791
Ministers' Returns p. 377.

2 March 1798. James ASHBROOK and Nancy Sims. Married by Rev.
James Rucks. Ministers' Returns p. 384.

19 February 1793. Jeremiah ASHBROOK and Rachel Baugh. Married
by Rev. Needler Robinson, Rector Dale Parish, Episcopal Church.
Ministers' Returns p. 377.

3 December 1811. John ASHTON and Mariah A. Buck, dau. of
Cornelius Buck who consents. Sur. Robert D. Murchie. p. 111.

14 August 1797. Pleasant ATKIN and Anne Gill. Married by Rev.
Needler Robinson, Rector Dale Parish, Episcopal Church. Ministers' Returns p. 385.

1801-1802. William ATKINS and Sarah Cunningham. Married by Rev
Eleazar Clay, Baptist. Ministers' Returns p. 394.

10 January 1779. Israel AUSTIN and Sarah Shaw. Sur. Colin
Fergusson. p. 8.

16 December 1802. William BABER and Susanna Johnson. Married
by Rev. Henry Featherstone, Sr. Ministers' Returns p. 396.

8 November 1783. John BADGETT and Milly Hatcher of lawful age.
Sur. George Markham. Wit. Mary Wadkins. Married 12 Nov. by Rev
William Hickman, Minister of Skinquarter Baptist Church. p. 19.

8 June 1783. Abram BAILEY and _____ _____. Sur. Benjamin
Baley. p. 18.

6

21 January 1789. James BAILEY and Elizabeth Lockett. Married by Rev. James Smith. Ministers' Returns p. 375.

_____ 1791. James BAILEY and Anne Lester. Married by Rev. Walthall Robertson, Baptist. Return dated 14 November 1791. Ministers' Returns p. 377.

25 November 1803. John BAILEY and Mary Bridgewater. Sur. James Ashbrook. Wit. Henry Bailey. p. 69.

2 September 1813. King BAILEY and Phebe Robertson, 21 years of age, dau. of James Robertson. Sur. Henry Roberts. p. 121.

23 January 1798. Obadiah BAILEY and Elizabeth Martin. Sur. Edward Nunnally. Wit. Thomas Finney. Married 27 January by Rev. James Rucks. p. 50.

13 September 1804. William BAILEY and Jane F. Flournoy. Sur. John Porter. See William Baley. p. 73.

19 November 1791. James BAIRD and Frances Cogbill. Married by Rev. John Cameron, Rector Bristol Parish, Episcopal Church.

_____ 1790. James BAKER and Margaret Morrissett. Married by Rev. Eleazer Clay, Baptist. Ministers' Returns p. 376.

5 June 1773. John BAKER and Doshea Sherrar. Nicholas Sherrar, guardian of Doshea, consents. Sur. Thomas Baker. Wit. George Sherer and Peter Day. p. 2.

4 June 1779. John BAKER and Elizabeth Cobbs. Sur. Thomas Bridgewater. p. 9.

29 August 1808. John BAKER and Tabitha Clarke, 21 years of age, dau. of Ellyson Clarke, Sr., deceased. Sur. Ellyson Clarke, Jr. Married by Rev. Eleazar Clay, Baptist, who says John Baker, Jr. p. 92.

10 October 1814. Matthew BAKER and Frances H. Wooldridge, 21 years of age, dau. of Daniel Wooldridge. Sur. John Hill. Married 11 October by Rev. Henry Bridgewater. p. 126.

1796-1797. Obadiah BAKER and Elizabeth Bowman. Married by Rev. Eleazer Clay, Baptist. Ministers' Returns p. 386.

20 January 1784. Thomas BAKER and Anne Elliott, dau. of Robert Ellett who consents. Sur. John Baker, Jr. Wit. George Markham. p. 20.

25 November 1786. William BAKER and Hany Brummall, dau. of William Brummall who consents. This is consent only. p. 24.

15 February 1813. William BALDWIN and Polly Alphin, 21 years of age. Sur. Nathaniel Forrester. p. 119.

11 February 1804. William BALEY and Jane F. Flournoy. Wit. John Porter and Thomas Flournoy. This is consent only. See William Bailey. p. 71.

13 August 1798. Isham BALL and Sally Hendrick, dau. of John Hendrick who consents. Wit. Daniel Weisiger and Richard Weisiger. This is consent only. p. 52.

_____ 1802. Valentine BALL and Mary Lockett. Married by Rev. Charles Forsee, Minister Skinquarter Baptist Church. Ministers' Returns p. 395.

2 October 1772. William BANTON and Frances Turpin. Sur. Henry Turpin. p. 1.

30 March 1793. John BARBER and Priscilla Evans. Married by Rev. John Cameron, Rector Bristol Parish, Episcopal Church.

21 September 1784. Philip BARBOUR and Ann Holt, of full age, dau. of David Holt. Sur. Thomas Holt. Philip Barbour's name also spelled Barber. p. 22.

21 August 1785. Thomas BARLOW and Elizabeth James. Married by Rev. William Leigh, Rector of Manchester Parish, Episcopal Church. "License in Borough of Petersburg." Ministers' Returns p. 370.

2 April 1804. John BARNER and Mary Elam, 21 years of age. Sur. John Flournoy. Married by Rev. Eleazar Clay, Baptist. p. 71.

14 July 1815. Thomas BARNES and Polly Goodwyn, dau. of Collins Goodwyn. Sur. Josiah T. Hudson. Wit. Lewellin Hudson. Married by Rev. Edmund Goode, Baptist. p. 130.

7 February 1778. Archibald BASS and Charlotte Stone. Sur. John Cogbill. p. 6.

_____ 1801. Arthur BASS and Judith Gates. Married by Rev. Charles Forsee, Minister of Skinquarter Baptist Church. Ministers' Returns p. 395.

24 August 1803. Christopher BASS and Phebe Cogbill. Sur. Peter Perry. p. 68.

1801-1802. Edward BASS and Pity Ellison. Married by Rev. Eleazar Clay, Baptist. Ministers' Returns p. 394.

22 June 1787. Joseph BASS and Mary Robertson, dau. of George Robertson who consents. Married 30 June by Rev. John Cameron, Rector of Bristol Parish. Episcopal Church. p. 26.

5 December 1790. Joseph BASS and Jenny Manlove. Married by Rev. Needler Robinson, Rector of Dale Parish, Episcopal Church. Ministers' Returns p. 375.

15 November 1799. Richard BASS and Nancy El___ (mutilated). Married by Rev. George Smith, Baptist. Ministers' Returns p. 387.

11 December 1810. Richard BASS and Elizabeth Farmer, dau. of Hezekiah Farmer who consents and is surety. p. 105.

18 August 1798. Thomas BASS and Sarah P. Bradley. Married by Rev. Needler Robinson, Rector of Dale Parish, Episcopal Church. Ministers' Returns p. 390.

2 January 1806. Thomas BASS and Phebe Cheatham. Married by Rev. Charles Forsee, Skinquarter Baptist Church. Mininsters' Returns p. 400.

7 April 1792. William BASS and Betsy Scott, dau. of Joseph Scott who consents. This is consent only. p. 34.

26 July 1813. William E. BASS and Lucy Finney Branch, dau. of Thomas Branch (deceased?). Samuel Jones, guardian of Lucy consents for her. Sur. Miles B. Branch. Wit. Jacob W. Branch and Edward H. Moseley. Married 29 July by Rev. Thomas Anderson. p. 120.

17 August 1811. Richard BATE and Violet Claiborne, widow. Sur. Richard McRae. p. 109.

6 November 1802. Chambling BATTE and Sarah Akin, dau. of Thomas Akin who consents. Wit. M. Walthall. p. 66.

5 June 1778. Thomas BATTE and Dorothy Baugh. Sur. Richard Baugh. p. 6.

19 January 1815. Thomas BATT and Clarissa B. Walthall, dau. of Henry Walthall, Sr. who consents and is surety. Wit. Chambling Batts. Married by Rev. Thomas Lafon, Church of Christ. p. 128.

15 April 1784. Amasa BAUGH and Patience Cheatham. Married by Rev. William Hickman, Minister of Skinquarter Baptist Church. Ministers' Returns p. 369.

29 December 1794. Andrew BAUGH and Nancy Britton. Sur. Thomas Britton. Nancy writes her own consent. p. 39.

5 December 1793. Archibald BAUGH and Sarah Worsham. Married b Rev. Needler Robinson, Rector of Dale Parish, Episcopal Church. Ministers' Returns p. 378.

2 November 1797. Archibald BAUGH and Rebecca Epps Worsham. Married by Rev. Needler Robinson, Rector of Dale Parish, Episco pal Church. Ministers' Returns p. 390.

7 January 1791. Daniel BAUGH and Ann Graves. Sur. Armistead Graves. Married by Rev. Eleazer Clay. p. 32.

8 September 1793. James BAUGH, Jr. and Dyson Norris. Sur. Samuel Clarke. Married by Rev. Eleazer Clay, Baptist. p. 37.

_____ _____ 1797. James BAUGH and Sarah Newby. Married by Rev Eleazar Clay, Baptist. She may have been Sarah Farguson m. 20 Nov. 1779 Levy Newby and m. 2nd James Baugh. See marriage of Lewis Puckett who married her dau. Rhody. Ministers' Returns p 392.

June 1788-June 1789. Jeremiah BAUGH and Mary Flournoy. Marrie by Rev. Eleazer Clay, Baptist. Ministers' Returns p. 373.

_____ _____ 1793. John BAUGH and Salley Rofret (?). Married b Rev. Eleazer Clay, Baptist. Ministers' Returns p. 381.

8 January 1810. John A. BAUGH and Anne Newby, dau. of Elisha Newby who consents. Sur. Martin Newby. p. 100.

22 October 1789. Joseph BAUGH and Martha Ashbrook. Sur. James Ashbrook. p. 29.

22 November 1813. Josiah BAUGH and Jinsey Fargusson, dau. of Joseph Fargusson who consents and is surety. Married 23 Novemb by Rev. Henry Bridgewater. p. 122.

4 June 1781. Peter BAUGH and Mary Ann Elam, dau. of James Elam who consents. Sur. William Blankenship. p. 14.

24 September 1805. Richard BAUGH and Prudence Elam, dau. of Samuel Elam who consents. Sur. John Baugh. Wit. William Elam. p. 78.

1 August 1809. Robart BAUGH and Judith Walthall. Married by Rev. Charles Forsee, Skinquarter Baptist Church. Ministers' Returns p. 402.

_____ 1809. Robertson BAUGH and Margaret Clarke. Married by Rev. Eleazar Clay, Baptist. Ministers' Returns p. 402.

13 December 1796. William BAUGH and Martha Walthall. Wit. William Dunn. This is consent only. Married by Rev. Needler Robinson, Rector of Dale Parish, Episcopal Church. p. 495.

24 November 1798. William BAUGH and Amey Crostick. Sur. Lewis Clarke. Married by Rev. Eleazer Clay, Baptist. p. 53.

24 November 1803. John BEASLEY and Nancy Goodwyn, dau. of Collins Goodwyn who consents. Married 26 November by Rev. Benjamin Watkins. p. 69.

20 September 1791. Stephen BEASLEY and Martha Cheatham, dau. of Thomas Cheatham who consents. This is consent only. Married by Rev. Eleazer Clay, Baptist, who says Patty. p. 33.

1801-1802. Thomas BEASLEY and Anne Dockett. Married by Rev. Eleazar Clay, Baptist. Ministers' Returns p. 394.

1803. William BEASLEY and Salley Hamblin. Married by Rev. Eleazar Clay, Baptist. Ministers' Returns p. 397.

10 November 1808. William BEASLEY and Rhoda Puckett, dau. of Nathaniel Puckett who consents and is surety. p. 93.

12 December 1810. Young BEASLEY and Anna Foulkes. Sur. Leonard Rudd. p. 105.

27 December 1780. Thomas BEDFORD and Anne Robertson. Sur. Thomas Walke. p. 13.

14 April 1806. Peter BEDLOCK and Martha Andress. Salley Andress consents for Martha. No relationship stated. Sur. William Andress. p. 81.

27 February 1786. Burwell BELCHER and Sarah Andrews. Married by Rev. William Leigh, Rector of Manchester Parish, Episcopal Church. Ministers' Returns p. 370.

18 March 1811. Daniel BELCHER and Dolly Graves. Consent of Arthur Graves for Dolly; no relationship stated. Sur. Thomas Graves, Jr. Wit. Matthew Graves. p. 107.

11 February 1811. Edmund BELCHER and Sally Andrews, dau. of Stephen and Mason Andrews who consent. Sur. Isham Belcher. Wit. Isham Belcher, Jr. and Robert Belcher. Married 20 February by Rev. Joseph Gill. p. 107.

28 May 1789. Isham BELCHER and Winifred Royall. Sur. Francis
Andrews. Wit. Grief Royall. Married 1 June by Rev. John
Cameron, Rector of Bristol Parish, Episcopal Church. p. 28.

12 October 1805. Isham BELCHER and Rachel Andrews, 21 years of
age, dau. of Stephen Andrews. Sur. Robert Andrews. Wit. Willia
Anderson. p. 78.

.30 July 1785. John Thomas BELCHER and Martha Jenkins. Married
by Rev. William Leigh. Rector of Manchester Parish, Episcopal
Church. Ministers' Returns p. 369.

7 October 1801. Morris BELCHER and Obedience Williams. Married
by Rev. Thomas Hardie, Methodist. Ministers' Returns p. 395.

23 April 1811. Robert BELCHER and Sally Fergusson, dau. of
William Fergusson who consents. Sur. John Fergusson. p. 108.

13 May 1815. Thomas BELCHER and Elizabeth Fergusson, dau. of
William Fergusson, Sr. Sur. William Freeman, Jr. Married 20 Ma
by Rev. Thomas Lafon, Church of Christ. p. 130.

26 January 1809. Eleazar BENNETT and Judith Jackson, 21 years
of age, dau. of Elizabeth Jackson. Sur. Hezekiah Bowman. p. 95

22 January 1803. Thomas BENNETT and Nancy Blankenship. Sur.
John Perkins. Wit. Abel Bowman. p. 66.

7 February 1815. David BENTON and Anney Walden, dau. of James
Walden, deceased. Sur. Obadiah Short. Married 9 February by
Rev. Thomas Lafon, Church of Christ who says <u>Ann</u>. p. 128.

27 November 1790. Creed BERRY and Mary Gill. Married by Rev.
Needler Robinson, Rector of Dale Parish, Episcopal Church.
Ministers' Returns p. 375.

4 February 1809. Daniel P. BERRY and Elizabeth Andrews, 21 year
of age, dau. of Stephen Andrews. Sur. Adam Andrews. Married
7 February by Rev. John Cox, Methodist. p. 95.

26 January 1786. David BERRY and Cilla Perkinson. Married by
Rev. William Leigh, Rector of Manchester Parish, Episcopal
Church. Ministers' Returns p. 370.

12

21 November 1785. James BERRY and Elizabeth Stewart. Married by Rev. William Leigh, Rector of Manchester Parish. Episcopal Church. Ministers' Returns p. 369.

2 February 1805. Peter BERRY and Lucy Graves. Married by Rev. Needler Robinson, Rector of Dale Parish, Episcopal Church. Ministers' Returns p. 391.

5 December 1799. William BERRY and Elizabeth Dance. Married by Rev. Needler Robinson, Rector of Dale Parish, Episcopal Church. Ministers' Returns p. 390.

10 July 1809. William BERRY and Patsey Dance, 21 years of age, dau. of John Dance, deceased. Sur. William Cousins. p. 97.

11 February 1807. Joseph BERTRAND and Mary Paul, dau. of Jurier Paul. Sur. William Watson Balding. Wit. Jessey Mims. p. 85.

22 February 1808. Joseph BERTRAND and Mary Smith, dau. of Benjamin Smith who consents and is surety. Wit. Sarah Smith. p. 89.

23 April 1792. John BEVERLEY and Mary Broadie. Sur. Archibald Broodie. p. 34.

1797-1798. Daniel BINS and Elizabeth Farmer. Married by Rev. Eleazer Clay, Baptist. Ministers' Returns p. 387.

20 April 1778. William BLACK Jr. and Elizabeth Trent, dau. of Alexander Trent who consents. Sur. John Archer. p. 6.

25 February 1783. Jesse BLACKWELL and Betty Smith, dau. of John and Elizabeth Smith whose consent is dated 25 Aug. 1783. Sur. James Nunnally - Jesse Blackwell of Goochland County. p. 18.

11 November 1813. Abraham BLANKENSHIP and Elizabeth Dance, dau. of William Dance who consents. Sur. Richard Taylor. Wit. Creed Berry. Married by Rev. Joseph Gill, Jr. p. 122.

10 April 1809. Archibald BLANKENSHIP and Nancy Totty, 21 years of age, dau. of Daniel Totty. Sur. Rowlett Deaton. Ministers' Returns dated 22 April say Mary Totty which is probably right. p. 96.

12 January 1790. Bland BLANKENSHIP and Lucy Moore. Married by Rev. John Cameron, Rector of Bristol Parish. Episcopal Church.

15 August 1792. Branch BLANKENSHIP and Sarah Fowler. Consent
of William Fowler for Sarah. No relationship stated. Wit.
Pleasant Fowler. This is consent only. Married by Rev. Eleaze
Clay, Baptist. p. 34.

9 April 1796. Branch BLANKENSHIP and Hannah Hancock. Sur.
William Traylor. Wit. Thomas Finney. Married by Rev. Eleazer
Clay, Baptist. p. 44.

1 April 1795. Burwell BLANKENSHIP and Phebe Russell. Sur.
Jeremiah Russell. Wit. Jeremiah Luster and Thomas Finney.
Married 4 April by Rev. James Rucks. p. 40.

18 June 1797. Burwell BLANKENSHIP and Judy Snellings, dau. of
Ann Morris who consents. Sur. William Roberts. Married by
Rev. James Rucks who says Judith Ann. p. 47.

25 December 1798. David BLANKENSHIP and Susannah Stringer.
Married by Rev. Nathan Anderson, Methodist. Ministers' Returns
p. 388.

11 August 1806. Emanuel BLANKENSHIP and Sarah Hobbs Walthall,
dau. of John Walthall, deceased. Sur. Henry Walthall. Married
14 August by Rev. Thomas Lafon, Church of Christ. p. 82.

6 October 1810. Ephraim BLANKENSHIP and Nancy J. Graves, 21
years of age. Consent of Cain Mann for Nancy; no relationship
stated. Sur. Abram Blankenship. p. 104.

2 March 1793. Ezekiel BLANKENSHIP and Reaney Charlton. Sur.
John Flournoy. Married 7 March by Rev. James Rucks. p. 36.

8 December 1785. George BLANKENSHIP and Fanny Moore. Married
Rev. William Leigh, Rector of Manchester Parish, Episcopal
Church. Ministers' Returns p. 370.

31 August 1808. George BLANKENSHIP and Polly Charleton, 21 yea
of age. Sur. Elam Farmer. Married 1 September by Rev. Charles
Forsee, Skinquarter Baptist Church. p. 92.

1797-1798. James BLANKENSHIP and Anne Railey. Married by Rev.
Eleazer Clay, Baptist. Ministers' Returns p. 387.

31 October 1789. Jesse BLANKENSHIP and Mica Moore. Sur. Bland
Blankenship. Wit. Philip Thweatt. Married 2 Nov. by Rev.
Needler Robinson, Rector of Dale Parish, Episcopal Church. p. 2

June 1788-June 1789. John BLANKENSHIP and Patsy Fowler. Marrie
by Rev. Eleazer Clay, Baptist. Ministers' Returns p. 373.

19 January 1786. Josiah BLANKENSHIP and Lucy Mann. Married by Rev. William Leigh, Rector of Manchester Parish, Episcopal Church. Ministers' Returns p. 370.

21 July 1812. Mackness BLANKENSHIP and Page Gates, dau. of Alexander and Mary Gates who consent. Sur. Jeremiah Nunnally. Wit. John Gates. p. 115.

4 December 1815. Mackness BLANKENSHIP and Rhoda Bowles. Sur. John Gates. Married 5 December by Rev. Edmund Goode, Baptist. p. 132.

27 May 1800. Nathan BLANKENSHIP and Ada Andrews, dau. of Simon Andrews who consents. Sur. Cain Mann. Wit. John Cary. p. 60.

28 March 1799. Pleasant BLANKENSHIP and Elizabeth Vaden. Married by Rev. Thomas Hardie, Methodist. Ministers' Returns p. 389.

_____ 1792. Stanton BLANKENSHIP and Susanna Perdue. Married by Rev. Eleazer Clay, Baptist. Ministers' Returns p. 379.

11 February 1782. Stephen BLANKENSHIP and Jean Hutcheson. Sur. Matthew Keys. p. 16.

18 January 1800. Sylvester BLANKENSHIP and Ann Wilson. Sur. Lodowick Puckett. Wit. John Cary. p. 59.

23 January 1795. Thomas BLANKENSHIP and Mary Smith. dau. of William Smith who consents. This is consent only. Married 24 January by Rev. Thomas Hardie, Methodist. p. 40.

2 November 1804. Thomas BLANKENSHIP and Jemima Robertson. Sur. Emanuel Blankenship. The bride's name is spelled Gemima. Married 3 November by Rev. Charles Hopkins. p. 74.

_____ 1793. Vincent BLANKENSHIP and Amasa Fowler. Married by Rev. Eleazer Clay, Baptist. Ministers' Returns p. 381.

_____ 1780. William BLANKENSHIP and _____ _____. Sur. Charles Hundley. p. 11.

23 September 1803. William BLANKENSHIP Jr. and Assenath Blankenship. Consent of William Blankenship, Sr. for both. Sur. Elam Farmer. Wit. George Blankenship. Married by Rev. James Rucks. p. 68.

9 December 1805. William BLANKENSHIP and Clarissa Smith, dau. William Smith who consents and is surety. Married 21 December by Rev. Thomas Lafon, Church of Christ. p. 79.

13 April 1807. William BLANKENSHIP and Polly Morris, dau. of John Morris. Sur. John Cheatham. Married 29 April by Rev. Charles Forsee, Skinquarter Baptist Church. p. 86.

1 November 1813. William BLANKENSHIP and Nancy Anderson. Sur. Thomas Anderson. Wit. Edward H. Anderson. Married 3 November by Rev. Jesse Lee. p. 122.

26 March 1796. Bartholomew BLUNT and Joanna Elam, dau. of James Elam. Married by Rev. Benjamin Watkins. p. 495.

22 January 1786. Daniel BOISSEAU and Priscilla Hill. Consent of Richard Covington, guardian of Priscilla. Wit. Thomas Cogbill. Married 28 Jan. by Rev. William Leigh, Rector of Manchester Parish, Episcopal Church. p. 24.

24 December 1801. David BOISSEAU and Tabitha Hatcher. Married by Rev. Thomas Hardie, Methodist. Ministers' Returns p. 395.

16 January 1798. Patrick BOISSEAU and Martha Winfrey. Married by Rev. Thomas Hardie, Methodist. Ministers' Returns p. 386.

13 October 1789. Fleming BOLES and Priscilla Gates. Sur. John Moody. Married by Rev. John Goode. See Fleming Bowles. p. 29

__ September 1783. Henry BOLES and Rachell Bailey, Sur. James Gates. Married 25 Oct. by Rev. William Hickman, Minister of Skinquarter Baptist Church. See Henry Bowles. p. 19.

16 July 1779. James BOLES and Rhoda Farmer. Sur. Jeremiah Nunnally. See James Bowles. p. 10.

__ August 1791. Thomas BOLES and Nancy Godsey, dau. of John Godsey who consents. This is consent only. p. 32.

6 February 1797. Thomas BOLES and Tabitha Farmer. Married by Rev. Nathan Anderson, Methodist. See Thomas Bowles. Ministers Returns p. 385.

16 December 1793. Lenias BOLLING and Mary Markham, not of age, dau. of Bernard Markham who consents. Sur. Robert Cary. Lenias Bolling of Buckingham County. p. 37.

16 May 1795. John BOMMAN and Mrs. Mary Tillotson. Wit. Jesse Tillotson. This is consent only. This name could be Bowman; old writing indistinct. p. 41.

14 November 1790. Richard BOOKER and Margaret McFarland. Married by Rev. John Cameron, Rector of Bristol Parish. Episcopal Church.

26 November 1802. Thomas BOOTH and Polly Winfree, of lawful age. Sur. Peter Franklin. Married by Rev. Eleazar Clay, Baptist. p. 66.

21 May 1801. Pleasants E. BOROUGH and Susannah Nobles. Married by Rev. Thomas Hardie, Methodist. Ministers' Returns p. 395.

11 August 1812. Archibald BOTT and Sally Gill, dau. of Joseph Gill, Jr. who consents. Sur. Daniel Gill. Wit. Epsey Gill. p. 115.

12 October 1795. Miles BOTTS, Jr. and Mary Beverley. Miles Bott, Jr. of Manchester. This is consent only. p. 42.

12 January 1801. Francis BOTTOM and Lucy Baker, dau. of John Baker who consents. This is consent only. p. 62.

22 April 1795. Reuben BOTTOM and Fanny Branch. Sur. Olive Hill (man). Wit. William Finney and Thomas Finney. Married by Rev. Eleazer Clay, Baptist. p. 41.

7 November 1814. Thomas BOTTOM and Mary W. Hall, 21 years of age. Sur. Bartlett Burton. Married 10 November by Rev. Thomas Lafon, Church of Christ. p. 126.

19 October 1808. Walker BOWLER and Edith Flournoy, dau. of William Flournoy, Sr. who consents. Sur. Peter Flournoy. Wit. John Porter. Married by Rev. Benjamin Watkins. p. 93.

13 October 1789. Fleming BOWLES and Priscilla Gates. See Fleming Boles. p. 485.

___ September 1783. Henry BOWLES and Rachael Bailey. See Henry Boles. p. 485.

16 July 1779. James BOWLES and Rhoda Farmer. Sur. Jeremiah Nunnally. See James Boles. p. 10.

24 October 1785. John BOWLES and Anne Haukins Landrum. Sur. Samuel Landrum. p. 23.

6 February 1797. Thomas BOWLES and Tabitha Farmer. Sur.
Alexander Sims. Wit. Daniel Ashbrook and William Finney. See
Thomas Boles. p. 47.

____ January 1802. Abel BOWMAN and Huldy Vaden. Married by Rev.
Thomas Hardie, Methodist. Ministers' Returns p. 395.

____ ____ 1789. Daniel BOWMAN and Mary Pilkinton. Married by
Rev. John Goode. Ministers' Returns p. 375.

8 March 1814. Edward BOWMAN and Betsey Otter, dau. of Kitty
Otter who consents. This is consent only. p. 124.

6 March 1805. Henry BOWMAN and Susannah Sims, widow of William
Sims Sur. Benjamin Jennings. Wit. Isaac Sallee', George F.
Sallee' and Anderson Sallee'. Married 7 March by Rev. Benjamin
Watkins. p. 75.

23 December 1808. Hezekiah BOWMAN and Lucy Jackson, 21 years of
age, dau. of Elizabeth Jackson. Sur. Francis Branch. p. 94.

17 November 1778. John BOWMAN and Lurina Cheatham. Sur. John
Perdue. p. 7.

____ ____ 1796. John BOWMAN and Mary Tilletson. Married by
Rev. Eleazer Clay, Baptist. Ministers' Returns p. 384.

1797-1799. Mackness BOWMAN and Agness Cunningham. Married by
Rev. Eleazer Clay, Baptist. Ministers' Returns p. 392.

14 August 1804. Thomas BRACKETT and Elizabeth Elam. Sur. Marle
Walthall. She must have been a widow. See marriage of John
Whitmore and Nancy Elam. p. 72.

1 October 1808. Caleb BRADLEY and Nancy Parry, dau. of William
Parry. Caleb Bradley is guardian of Nancy. Sur. Marvil Winfree
p. 92.

13 August 1798. John Royal BRADLEY and Mary Archer. William
Archer, guardian of Mary consents for her; no relationship
stated. This is consent only. Married 14 August by Rev. Needle
Robinson, Rector of Dale Parish, Episcopal Church. p. 52.

1 February 1775. William BRADLEY and Sisley Johnson, dau. of
William Johnson. Wit. Benjamin Watkins. This is consent only.
p. 4.

1797-1799. Joel BRAGG and Elizabeth Furguson. Married by Rev.
Eleazer Clay, Baptist. Ministers' Returns p. 392.

27 December 1806. John BRAGG and Polly Deaton, dau. of John
Deaton, deceased, and Mary Deaton, who consents. Sur. Rowlett
Deaton. Wit. Woodson Vaden. p. 84.

_____ 1790. William BRAGG and Masey Furguson. Married by
Rev. Eleazer Clay, Baptist. Ministers' Returns p. 376.

20 April 1786. Archer BRANCH and Mary Bernard, dau. of William
Bernard who consents. Wit. J. Bolling, Jr. and Robert Bernard.
This is consent only. Same as next marriage. Married 28 June
by Rev. William Leigh, Rector of Manchester Parish, Episcopal
Church. p. 24.

8 June 1786. Archer BRANCH and Mary Bernard. William Fleming
consents for Mary bearing date 8 June 1786. Wit. Henry Archer
and Henry Elam. This is consent only. Married 28 June by Rev.
William Leigh, Rector of Manchester Parish, Episcopal Church.
p. 24.

25 August 1773. Benjamin BRANCH and Mazy Branch. No surety.
p. 2.

1 December 1780. Benjamin BRANCH and Betty Epes Osborne. Sur.
George Markham. p. 13.

19 February 1800. Bolling BRANCH and Rebecca Graves, dau. of
Arthur Graves who consents. Sur. Thomas Branch. p. 59.

15 December 1783. Edward BRANCH and Ann Eppes. Sur. Benjamin
Branch. p. 19.

June 1786-June 1787. Edward BRANCH and Tabitha Horner. Married
by Rev. Eleazer Clay, Baptist. Ministers' Returns p. 372.

26 December 1808. Henry BRANCH and Elizabeth Haskins. Married
by Rev. Charles Forsee, Skinquarter Baptist Church. Ministers'
Returns p. 401.

10 June 1799. James BRANCH and Polly Hancock, dau. of Ananias
Hancock who consents. Sur. Archibald Short. Married 15 June
by Rev. Benjamin Watkins. p. 55.

13 January 1798. Joseph BRANCH and Susanna Branch. Married by
Rev. Nathan Anderson, Methodist. Ministers' Returns p. 388.

6 July 1799. Olive BRANCH and Sally Ash, dau. of John Ash who
consents. Sur. Edward Bennett. Wit. Henry Winfree, James Roper
and Ossimus Warner. Married by Rev. Benjamin Watkins. p. 55.

31 December 1790. Peter BRANCH and Polly Cheatham, dau. of
Thomas Cheatham, Sr. who consents. Sur. Thomas Short, Jr. p.

19 December 1811. Robert F. BRANCH and Mary Tatum, dau. of
Henry Tatum who consents. Sur. Parke Poindexter. p. 111.

15 September 1807. Washington BRANCH and Polley Brechan, 21
years of age, dau. of Jusia Brechan. Sur. Robert Allen. p. 87.

24 February 1812. Hector BRANDER and Eliza Brander, dau. of
John Brander who consents. Sur. Daniel Foster. Wit. John Perry
p. 112.

19 March 1791. John BRANDER and Martha Field Robertson. Marrie
by Rev. Needler Robinson, Rector of Dale Parish, Episcopal
Church. Ministers' Returns p. 375.

16 December 1812. William BRANSFORD and Frances Hundley, 21
years of age, dau. of Charles Hundley. Sur. Wiley Jackson.
p. 118.

18 March 1787. Larkin BRANSOM and Tabitha Cheatham. Sur. John
Radford. Married by Rev. Eleazer Clay, Baptist. p. 25.

28 May 1798. Jeremiah BRAUGHTON and Anne Womack. Sur. John
Edmonds. Married by Rev. Walthall Robertson, Baptist. Return
dated 2 June 1799. p. 52.

8 October 1803. Samuel BRIDGEWATER and Nancy Bailey. Sur. James
Ashbrook. Wit. James Gates and Sally Gates. Married by Rev.
James Rucks. p. 69.

_____ 1793. Thomas BRIDGEWATER and Obedience Hancock.
Married by Rev. James Smith. Ministers' Returns p. 379.

_____ 1793. John BRIGGS and Anne Lockett. Married by
Rev. Eleazer Clay, Baptist. Ministers' Returns p. 381.

15 April 1807. William BRIGHTWELL and Salley Turner, widow of
John Turner. Sur. Peter Finney. p. 86.

10 February 1806. Jacob BRINTLE, Jr. and Patsey Nunnally, 21 years of age, dau. of David Nunnally, deceased. Sur. Charles Nunnally. p. 81.

11 December 1802. William BRITTAIN and Maxea Moore. Married by Rev. Needler Robinson, Rector of Dale Parish, Episcopal Church. Ministers' Returns p. 391.

19 December 1815. Anderson BRITTON and Lucy Jackson, dau. of Abel Jackson, deceased. Sur. John W. Gill. Married 21 December by Rev. Joseph Gill, Jr. p. 132.

25 January 1784. John BRITTON and Martha Eanes. Wit. Edward Eanes. This is consent only. p. 20.

25 January 1800. Thomas BRITTON and Polly Eanes, dau. of William Eanes who consents. Sur. Abraham Burton. Wit. John Cary. p. 59.

10 November 1806. William BRITTON and Pamelia K. Wells. Sur. William C. Wells. p. 83.

9 June 1803. Daniel BROADIE and Sally Henedge. Sur. Jesse Hix. p. 67.

2 April 1779. Christopher BROOKE and Agnes Adams. Sur. Nathaniel Quarles. Wit. John Puller. See Christopher Brooks. p. 9.

2 April 1779. Christopher BROOKS and Agnes Adams. Sur. Nathaniel Quarles. Wit. John Fuller. See Christopher Brooke. o. 9.

11 March 1780. Elias BROOKS and Moley Hix, dau. of John and Ruth Hix who consent. Sur. Peter Varnier. Wit. Elizabeth Fair Bush. p. 11.

12 June 1805. Elias BROOKS and Elizabeth Brooks, 21 years of age, dau. of William Brooks, deceased. Sur. William Hix. Married by Rev. Charles Hopkins. p. 77.

10 February 1807. Elias BROOKS and Phebe Farmer, 21 years of age. Elizabeth Farmer consents for Phebe; no relationship stated. Sur. Archer Farmer. Wit. Fanny Farmer and Mary Farmer. p. 85.

11 May 1798. Jeremiah BROOKS and Elizabeth Googer, dau. of Elizabeth Googer who consents. Wit. Lewis Lester and Andrew Martin Goodger. This name may be Goocher or Goodger. Tis is consent only. p. 51.

11 January 1790. John BROOKS and Phebe Lockett. Sur. Edward
Branch. Wit. Philip Thweat. p. 30.

16 February 1804. Joshua BROOKS and Sarah Baker, Jr., dau. of
Martin Baker who consents. Sur. Archer Farmer. p. 71.

_____ 1792. Martin BROOKS and Anne Snellings. Married by
Rev. Eleazer Clay, Baptist. Ministers' Returns p. 379.

4 November 1815. Silas Brooks and Judith Hix. Both 21 years of
age. Sur. Thomas Snellings. Married By Rev. Daniel Hudson.
p. 131.

14 February 1792. Thomas BROOKS and Fanny Branch. Wit. Olive
Hill. This is consent only. Married by Rev. James Smith. p. 3

3 January 1791. William BROOKS and Patty Cheatham, dau. of
Richard Cheatham. Sur. John Atkinson. Wit. W. Finney. p. 32.

10 September 1796. John BROWDER and Betsy Dyson. This is
consent only. Married 29 September by Rev. Thomas Hardie,
Methodist. p. 45.

15 February 1813. Richard BROWDER and Elizabeth Anderson. Sur.
Thomas Anderson. Wit. Edward W. Anderson. Married 24 February
by Rev. Hezekiah McLelland. p. 119.

7 February 1814. Dudley BROWN and Polley Chalkley, 22 years of
age. Sur. Seth Chalkley; no relationship stated. Wit. John
Kelly. Married 8 February by Rev. Thomas Lafon, Church of
Christ. p. 124.

19 January 1810. Garrot BROWN and Frances Horner, dau. of
Nathan Horner, deceased. Sur. William Beasley. Married 22
January by Rev. Thomas Lafon, Church of Christ who says Garret.
p. 100.

8 October 1804. Herbert BROWN and Mary Hill. Sur. James Moody.
Wit. Pleasant Barrow. p. 73.

23 June 1808. Jesse Brown and Mary Rowlett Partin, dau. of
John Partin who consents. Sur. Herbert Brown. Wit. William S.
Dance, Dennis Partin and Robert Partin. Married 25 June by Rev.
John Cox, Methodist. p. 91.

19 September 1794. Joel BROWN and Retty Gill. Married by Rev.
Thomas Hardie, Methodist. Ministers' Returns p. 382.

12 May 1790. John BROWN and Elizabeth Hatcher. Married by Rev. Needler Robinson, Rector of Dale Parish, Episcopal Church. Ministers' Returns p. 375.

18 January 1813. John BROWN and Sophia Farmer, dau. of Peter Farmer who consents. Married 19 January by Rev. Thomas Lafon, Church of Christ. p. 118.

21 December 1794. Armstreat BRUCE and Martha Hatcher, dau. of Samuel Hatcher who consents. Wit. Benjamin Hatcher and Archibald Hatcher. This is consent only. Married by Rev. Thomas Hardie, Methodist. Returned 1 Jan. 1795. p. 39.

14 September 1801. Benjamin BRUMMAL and Sally Paull, dau. of Elizabeth Skelton who consents. Wit. Isaac Skelton. This is consent only. p. 63.

23 November 1799. John BRUMMALL and Elizabeth Gregory, dau. of Thomas Gregory who consents. Sur. John Gregory. p. 56.

11 June 1804. Reuben BRUMMALL and Wealthy Ann Ellett, 21 years of age, dau. of Cornelius Ellett who consents. Sur. William Ellett. Married 14 June by Rev. Benjamin Watkins who says Elliot. p. 72.

14 May 1812. Royall BRUMMALL and Barbara Baugh. Sur. John Hix. p. 114.

20 February 1787. William BRUMMALL and Maryan Cox, dau. of Higginson Cox who consents. This is consent only. p. 25.

27 November 1809. Silas BRYANT and Janette Blounty, dau. of Thompson Blount who consents. Sur. Thomas Blount. p. 99.

17 December 1796. Lewis BUCKNER and Mrs. Susanna Lepnor. Sur. Ludwell Leneve. Wit. Sterling Norvell (or Nowell). p. 45.

June 1786-June 1787. John BULLOCK and Elizabeth Railey. Married by Rev. Eleazer Clay, Baptist. Ministers' Returns p. 372.

23 March 1799. William BURCH and Anne Hollidge. Married by Rev. Thomas Hardie, Methodist. Ministers' Returns p. 389.

14 August 1815. Joseph BURFOOT and Elizabeth Hardie Howlett, dau. of James Howlett who consents and is surety. Joseph is son of Thomas Burfoot, Sr. who consents for him. Married 24 August by Rev. Thomas Lafon, Church of Christ. p. 130.

13 December 1803. Lawson BURFOOT and Martha S. Clay, dau. of
Eleazar Clay who consents. Wit. Matthew Clay and Levinia Clay.
p. 69.

9 September 1811. Matthew BURFOOT and Mary E. Trabue, dau. of
Daniel Trabue who consents and is surety. p. 109.

15 March 1805. Thomas BURFOOT and Mary Bass. Married by Rev.
Charles Hopkins. Ministers' Returns p. 398.

28 October 1793. William BURKE and Lucy Bryers, dau. of Lucy
Bryers who consents. Wit. Thomas Bryers and Archer Webber.
This is consent only. Married by Rev. James Smith of Powhatan
County. p. 37.

2 June 1797. Edward BURNETT and Rhody Roper, dau. of Joseph
Roper who consents. Wit. Elizabeth Roper and William Pool. Thi
is consent only. Married 3 June by Rev. Benjamin Watkins.
p. 47.

28 August 1804. Henry BURNETT and Judith Cary, 21 years of age,
dau. of Mary Cary who consents. Sur. Henry Cary. Married 1
September by Rev. Benjamin Watkins. p. 73.

27 March 1801. James BURNETT and Milly Russell, dau. of Frances
Russell who consents. Wit, Phebe Pool and Field Russel. This
is consent only. p. 62.

15 January 1800. Arthur BURTON and Nancy Dance. Married by
Rev. Needler Robinson, Rector of Dale Parish, Episcopal Church.
Ministers' Returns p. 390.

25 January 1800. Bartlett BURTON and Elizabeth Newell. Sur.
Abraham Burton. Wit. John Cary. p. 59.

16 January 1798. Charles BURTON and Anne Cousins. Married by
Rev. Thomas Hardie, Methodist. Ministers' Returns p. 386.

7 February 1801. Charles BURTON and Elizabeth Branch, dau. of
Edward Branch, Senr. who consents. Wit. Edward Branch. This
is consent only. Married 26 February by Rev. Benjamin Watkins.
p. 62.

12 March 1810. Jesse W. BURTON and Polly Franklin, dau. of Joel
Franklin who consents. Sur. James Pride. Wit. Edmund Burton
and J. Y. Covington. p. 100.

6 August 1775. John BURTON and Sarah Horner. Sur. William
Walthall. p. 4.

21 August 1777. John BURTON and Sarah Elam. Sur. Robert Burton. Wit. George Elam. p. 5.

24 September 1779. John BURTON and Mary Gordon. Sur. John B. Forsie or Forsee. p. 10.

5 October 1809. John BURTON and Sally Burton, 21 years of age, dau. of John Burton, deceased. Sur. Obadiah Cox. p. 98.

29 March 1793. Joseph BURTON and Phebe Haskins, dau. of Robert Haskins who consents. This is consent only. Married 6 April by Rev. George Smith, Baptist. p. 36.

__ December 1781. Richard BURTON and ____ _____. Sur. John Burton. p. 15.

19 January 1797. Robert BURTON and Sarah Perkins. Married by Rev. Needler Robinson, Rector of Dale Parish. Episcopal Church. Ministers' Returns p. 385.

5 July 1774. Thomas BURTON and Sarah Cheatham. Sur. William Cheatham. p. 3.

2 October 1772. William BURTON and Frances Turpin. p. 485.

26 November 1811. William BURTON and Susanna Rigsby, dau. of Henry Rigsby who consents. Sur. John Burton. Married 28 November by Rev. Benjamin Watkins. p. 110.

18 May 1784. James BUSKITT and Mrs. Mildred Wade. Consent of David Wade for Mildred. Sur. John Hix. p. 21.

20 October 1792. Jesse BUTLER and Margaret Goode. Sur. Benjamin Goode. p. 34.

16 December 1807. Dr. R. B. CABELL and Elizabeth Walthall, dau. of Frances Walthall. Sur. Edward Archer. p. 88.

6 October 1810. William CAIN and Sarah Smith, dau. of Benjamin Smith who consents and is surety. Married 16 October by Rev. Benjamin Devany. p. 104.

6 August 1791. Joseph CALVIN and Elizabeth Wells. Married by Rev. John Cameron, Rector of Bristol Parish, Episcopal Church.

20 December 1814. Joseph CARDO and Elizabeth Elam, 21 years of age, dau. of Judith Elam who consents. Sur. William Ellyson. p. 127.

29 April 1779. Francis CARDWELL and Theodosha Wager Platt, dau. of Henson Platt who consents. Sur. Richard Cardwell. p. 9.

10 October 1814. Levi CARPENTER and Betsey Nunnally. Sur. Thomas Shell. Married 15 October by Rev. Thomas Lafon, Church of Christ. p. 126.

30 September 1803. John CARR and Susanna Stith Cogbill. See John Kerr. p. 485.

5 January 1803. James CARTER and Pheaba Farmer. Married by Rev. Charles Forsee, Minister of Skinquarter Baptist Church. Ministers' Returns p. 393.

10 December 1792. Edward CARY and Sally Butler. This is consent only. Married by Rev. James Smith. p. 35.

13 August 1810. Edward CARY and Nancy Bowman, dau. of Daniel Bowman who consents and is surety. p. 103.

1 April 1786. John CARY and Sarah Loofman. Married by Rev. John Goode. Ministers' Returns p. 371.

27 April 1790. Kemp CARY and Rebecca Butler. Sur. John Cary. Wit. Philip Thweatt and William Moseley. Married by Rev. James Smith. Return dated Manakin Town 10 March 1791. p. 30.

_____ 1791. Miles CARY and Obedience Brummall. Married by Rev. James Smith. Return dated 10 March 1791, Manakin Town. Ministers' Returns p. 377.

30 July 1903. Nathaniel CARY and Frances Morrisette, dau. of William Morrissett, granddau. of William Farrar. Sur. William Hix. Wit. Nelson Farrar and Thomas Blunt. p. 92.

26 January 1795. Peter Minor CARY and Rhoda Cox, dau. of Mary Cox who consents. Sur. John Weisiger. Married 31 January by Rev. Benjamin Watkins. p. 40.

13 May 1793. Robert CARY and Mary Ann Branch, dau. of Edward Branch who consents. This is consent only. Married by Rev. James Smith. p. 37.

___ _____ 1793. Wilson CARY and Judith Baker. Married by Rev. James Smith. Ministers' Returns p. 379.

10 December 1785. Joel CASHION and Martha Jackson. Married by Rev. William Leigh, Rector of Manchester Parish, Episcopal Church. Ministers' Returns p. 370.

26 February 1795. Tho(mas) CASHION. Sr. and Sarah Jackson. Married by Rev. Nathan Anderson, Methodist. Ministers' Returns p. 380.

30 September 1803. Thomas CAVENDER and ____ Bailey, dau. of Abram Bailey who consents. Wit. Jeremiah Bailey and Archer Bailey. This is consent only. p. 68.

____ ____ 1792. Riley CAYCE and Nancy Hubard. Married by Rev. Eleazer Clay, Baptist. Ministers' Returns p. 380.

10 September 1781. Archibald CAYCEY and Phebe Farmer. Sur. Robert Adkins. Wit. Vaul Cunningham. (This was Valentine Cunningham.) p. 14.

11 January 1795. John CAYSEY and Mary Sims. Married by Rev. James Rucks. Ministers' Returns p. 383.

CHALKLEY: See CHAULKLY

23 April 1811. Bartlett CHALKLEY and Martha Horner. Sur. Horatio Farmer. p. 108.

16 March 1785. Benjamin CHALKLEY and Sally Blankenship. Sur. Thomas Sadler. p. 22.

20 September 1811. Branch CHALKLEY and Rachel G. Gardner, dau. of Henry Gardner who consents. Sur. Nelson Winfree. p. 109.

17 January 1801. Daniel CHALKLEY and Ann Grigory. Sur. John Grigory. Wit. John Cary. Married by Rev. Eleazer Clay, Baptist. p. 62.

13 September 1785. David CHALKLEY and Elizabeth Smith. Married by Rev. William Leigh, Rector of Manchester Parish, Episcopal Church. Ministers' Returns p. 369.

15 March 1786. Elijah CHALKLEY and Dicey Farmer. Married by Rev. William Leigh, Rector of Manchester Parish, Episcopal Church. Ministers' Returns p. 370.

19 January 1793. Seth CHALKLEY and Prudence Horner. Married by Rev. Thomas Hardie, Methodist. Ministers' Returns p. 380.

20 November 1780. Robert CHAPPELL and Elizabeth Simm, 21 years of age. Sur. Edward Archer. Wit. William Rowlett. Married by Rev. William Harrison, Rector of Bristol Parish. Return dated 12 Nov. p. 12.

18 October 1804. Thomas CHATHAM and Salley Ellis, 21 years of age. Sur. William Ellis. p. 74.

14 May 1804. Obed CHAULKLEY and Nancy Adkins, dau. of Robert
Adkins who consents. Sur. George Adkins. p. 72.

23 December 1803. Abijah CHEATHAM and ____ Akin, dau. of
Arthur Akin who consents. Wit. Pleasant Cheatham. This is
consent only. p. 70.

24 October 1796. Archer CHEATHAM and Margaret Rudd. Sur.
Samuel Cheatham. Wit. Burnett Brown. Married by Rev. Nathan
Anderson, Methodist. p. 45.

19 December 1793. Benjamin CHEATHAM and Tabitha Moseley, dau.
Alexander Moseley who consents. Sur. William Cheatham. Marrie
21 December by Rev. James Rucks. p. 38.

23 February 1778. Bernard CHEATHAM and Margaret Cheatham. Sur
Hezekiah Turpin. p. 6.

12 December 1785. Barnard CHEATHAM and Ann Rudd, dau. of Thoma
Rudd, Jr. who consents. Married 15 Dec. by Rev. John Goode who
says Bernard. p. 23.

Probably 1792. Bernard CHEATHAM and Lucy Robertson. Married b
Rev. Walthall Robertson, Baptist. Ministers' Returns p. 379.

3 March 1796. Christopher CHEATHAM and Rebecca B. Cheatham.
Sur. William Cheatham, Jr. p. 43.

31 January 1814. Daniel CHEATHAM and Martha Branch. Thompson
Blunt, guardian of Martha, consents for her. Sur. George W.
Cole. Wit. Haley Cole. p. 124.

13 May 1812. Elam CHEATHAM and Elizabeth Powell. Sur. Robert
Baugh. Wit. Mary Moore. p. 114.

1801-1802. Eleazar CHEATHAM and Martha Roberson. Married by
Rev. Eleazar Clay, Baptist. Ministers' Returns p. 394.

23 December 1814. Francis CHEATHAM and Nancy Flournoy, 21 year
of age, dau. of James Flournoy. John Farley, guardian of Franc
Cheatham. Sur. Seth W. Flournoy. Wit. King Lockett and John P.
Crump. Married 24 Dec. by Rev. Edmund Goode, Baptist. p. 127.

27 July 1789. Henry CHEATHAM, Jr. and Mary Lockett. Sur. Ishan
Cheatham. p. 28.

19 December 1812. Henry CHEATHAM and Sosha Nunnally, dau. of
Edward Nunnally who consents and is surety. Pleasant Cheatham
consents for Henry; no relationship stated. p. 118.

10 October 1793. Hezekiah CHEATHAM and Lucy Brooks, dau. of William and Rebecca Brooks who consent. Elizabeth Cheatham, mother of Hezekiah. consents for him. This is consent only. Married by Eleazer Clay, Baptist. p. 37.

10 May 1797. Hezekiah CHEATHAM and Elizabeth Bowman, dau. of Daniel and Sarah Bowman who consent. Wit. Hezekiah Bowman and Mary Bowman. This is consent only. Married by Rev. Eleazer Clay, Baptist. p. 47.

7 April 1775. Isham CHEATHAM and Phebe Elam. Sur. James Elam. p. 4.

18 December 1806. Isham CHEATHAM and Hannah Spears, dau. of John Spears who consents. Sur. Thomas Bass, Jr. Wit. William Goode and Tapley Goode. William Goode guardian of Isham. Married by Rev. Charles Forsee, Minister of Skinquarter Baptist Church. p. 83.

25 August 1799. James CHEATHAM and Frances Ellyson, dau. of Milly Ellyson who consents. Sur. William Hix. Wit. Archibald Wooldridge. Married by Rev. Benjamin Watkins. p. 56.

12 November 1789. Josiah CHEATHAM and Rebecca Morgan, dau. of John Morgan who consents. This is consent only. Married by Rev. Eleazer Clay, Baptist. p. 29.

14 February 1793. Josiah CHEATHAM and Ann Walthall. Married by Rev. James Rucks. Ministers' Returns p. 378.

11 September 1788. Leonard CHEATHAM and Mary Walthall, dau. of Richard Walthall who consents. This is consent only. Married by Rev. John Goode. p. 27.

30 January 1798. Leonard CHEATHAM and Nancy Shackleford, dau. of Edward Bass who consents. (Step-father?) Sur. Richard Elam. Wit. T. Watkins. Married 3 February by Rev. George Smith. Baptist. p. 50.

9 May 1793. Matthew CHEATHAM and Martha Sherwin. William Cryer of Nottoway County consents for Martha. Wit. John Pegram, Jr. and Thomas Booth. This is consent only. Married 12 May by Rev. Needler Robinson, Rector of Dale Parish, Episcopal Church. p. 36.

21 December 1807. Matthew CHEATHAM and Elizabeth G. Elam, dau. of Richard Elam who consents. Sur. James Elam. Married by Rev. Charles Forsee, Skinquarter Baptist Church. p. 88.

29

24 January 1797. Peter CHEATHAM and Sally Cheatham. Sur. Samuel Cheatham. Wit. Thomas Finney. Married 2 February by Rev. Nathan Anderson, Methodist. p. 46.

18 December 1805. Pleasant CHEATHAM and Martha Walthall, dau. of William Walthall who consents. Sur. Francis Cheatham. Married by Rev. Charles Forsee, Minister of Skinquarter Baptist Church. p. 80.

23 September 1811. Richard CHEATHAM and Phebe W. Porter, dau. of John Porter who consents. Sur. Isaac D. Porter. Wit. John Porter, Jr. Married 26 September by Rev. Jordan Martin. p. 110

10 February 1789. Robertson CHEATHAM and Martha Ellett. Married by Rev. James Smith. Ministers' Returns p. 375.

18 October 1792. Samuel CHEATHAM and Nancy Rudd. Married by Rev. Walthall Robertson, Baptist. Ministers' Returns p. 379.

1797-1799. Stephen CHEATHAM and Wine Hudson. Married by Rev. Eleazer Clay, Baptist. Ministers' Returns p. 392.

11 August 1812. Thomas CHEATHAM and Eliza Bruce, dau. of Armstreat Bruce who consents. Sur. Peter F. Edwards. Wit. William Brummall and Stephen Branch. p. 115.

25 May 1790. William CHEATHAM and Pheby Ellis. Sur. Joel Cheatham. p. 30.

10 December 1814. William CHEATHAM and Jane Foulkes, 21 years of age. Sur. Samuel Cheatham. Married 15 December by Rev. Thomas Anderson, Sr. p. 127.

15 July 1808. Daniel CHEATWOOD and Winney Lockett, 21 years of age, dau. of Gideon Lockett, deceased. Sur. Thomas Porter. Married 21 July by Rev. Benjamin Watkins. p. 92.

1 April 1812. John T. CHILDERS and Mary Traylor, dau. of Mial Traylor who consents. Sur. Vaden Moore. Wit. James Smith. John son of Meredith Childers. Married 2 April by Rev. Joseph Gill, Jr.

30 June 1791. Maradith CHILDERS and Polly Tomes, dau. of Benjamin Toms who consents. Sur. Thomas Block. p. 32.

28 May 1795. Bathurst CLAIBORNE and Betsey Ann Bott. John Bott consents for Betsy Ann; no relationship stated. This is consent only. Married by Rev. Needler Robinson, Rector of Dale Parish, Episcopal Church.

9 August 1796. Bathurst CLAIBORNE and Mary Leigh Claiborne, dau. of William Claiborne of Falls Plantation who consents. Bathurst Claiborne b. 6 April 1774, son of Augustine Claiborne and Mary Herbert. p. 44.

10 June 1807. William CLARE and Rebecca Horsley, dau. of James Horsley who consents and is surety. See William Clarke; given both ways on same page. p. 86.

_____ 1803. Charles CLARK and Elizabeth Miller. Married by Rev. Eleazar Clay, Baptist. Ministers' Returns p. 397.

_____ 1796. James CLARK and Sarah Newby. Married by Rev. Eleazer Clay, Baptist. Ministers' Returns p. 384.

21 October 1805. James CLARK, Jr. and Martha Harrison Murchie, dau. of John Murchie who consents. Sur. Parke Poindexter. p. 79.

23 November 1795. Lewis CLARK and Polly Moxley. Sur. Rowland Puckett. Wit. Thomas Finney. Married by Rev. Eleazer Clay, Baptist. p. 42.

1796-1797. Samuel CLARK and Ann Winfrey. Married by Rev. Eleazer Clay, Baptist. Ministers' Returns p. 386.

11 November 1790. William CLARK and Mary Ann Hare, dau. of Parker Hare who consents. This is consent only. Married 25 December by Rev. John Cameron, Rector of Bristol Parish, Episcopal Church. p. 31.

2 May 1799. Allyson CLARKE and Elizabeth Coates, 21 years of age, dau. of John Coates who consents. Sur. William Coates. Wit. Gardner Clarke and Rhoda Coates. See Ellison Clarke, p. 55.

7 May 1779. Charles CLARKE and Nancy Martin. Sur. Daniel Trabue. p. 9.

_____ 1797. Ellison CLARKE and Elizabeth Coats. Married by Rev. Eleazer Clay, Baptist. See Allyson Clarke. Ministers' Returns p. 392.

26 September 1812. Frederick CLARKE and Maria E. Bott, dau. of Miles Bott who consents. Sur. William E. Clarke. Wit. W. Archer. p. 116.

12 January 1795. James CLARKE and Nancy Hancock, dau. of Francis Hancock who consents. Wit. John Clarke. This is consent only. Married 13 January by Rev. Benjamin Watkins. p. 40.

18 December 1804. James CLARKE and Frances Newby. Sur. John Clarke and Francis Clarke. p. 74.

4 December 1812. Jeremiah CLARKE and Martha Lester, 21 years of age, dau. of Jeremiah Lester. Sur. Daniel Wilkinson. p. 117.

15 October 1791. John CLARKE and Elizabeth H. Moseley, dau. of Edward Moseley who consents. Sur. Robert Wooldridge. Wit. John Brummall. p. 33.

_____ 1785. Joseph CLARKE and Dinah Newby. Sur. Jesse Clarke. p. 495.

25 January 1806. Peter CLARKE and Susanna Perdue, 21 years of age, dau. of Ezekiel Perdue, deceased, and Mary Perdue. Sur. Beville Archer. p. 80.

9 January 1809. Peter CLARKE, Sr. and Elizabeth Moore, dau. of Eleazar Moore, deceased. Sur. John Perdue. Married by Rev. Eleazar Clay, Baptist. p. 95.

18 November 1811. Shadrach CLARKE and Cally Akin, dau. of James Akin who consents and is surety. p. 110.

22 December 1792. Thomas CLARKE and Sophia Bevel. Married by Rev. John Lee, Methodist. Ministers' Returns p. 381.

18 October 1804. William B. CLARKE and Alice (or Alsey) Graves, dau. of Arthur Graves who consents. Sur. Matthew Graves. p. 7.

10 June 1807. William CLARKE and Rebecca Horsley, dau. of James Horsley who consents and is surety. See William Clare; given both ways on same page. p. 86.

4 December 1787. James M. CLARREN and Martha Berry. Married by Rev. John Cameron, Rector of Bristol Parish, Episcopal Church.

20 January 1813. Phineas CLAY and Frances Williamson Turpin. Sur. Henry Turpin. Married 21 January by Rev. Thomas Lafon, Church of Christ. p. 118.

3 March 1802. Samuel CLAY and Martha Burfoot, dau. of Thomas Burfoot who consents. p. 65.

26 April 1784. William CLAYBROOK and Lovina Ashurst. Sur. Josiah Jackson. Married 28 April by Rev. William Hickman who says Lorana Ashurst. William Hickman was Minister of Skinquarter Baptist Church. p. 21.

17 March 1785. Thomas B. CLAYTON and Obedience Sudbury. Wit. Ezekiel Sudbury. This is consent only. p. 22.

8 March 1813. Thomas CLAYTON and Sarah Varnier, dau. of John Varnier who consents and is surety. p. 119.

14 September 1795. George CLEATON and Sarah Mann. Married by Rev. Needler Robinson, Rector of Dale Parish. Episcopal Church. Ministers' Returns p. 378.

4 August 1807. James CLOPTON and Martha Winfree, dau. of William Winfree, deceased. Samuel Clarke, guardian of Martha consents for her and is surety. p. 86.

5 August 1799. James CLIBORNE and Elizabeth Elam, dau. of Lucy Elam who consents. Sur. Daniel Cliborne. Wit. John Rudd and William Worsham. p. 56.

20 August 1786. William CLYBORNE and Sally Frith. Sur. Leonard Clyborne. (I think this name was Cleborne.) p. 24.

25 March 1795. John COATS and Tabitha Cheatham. Married by Rev. Nathan Anderson, Methodist. Ministers' Returns p. 383.

4 November 1797. William COATES and Rhoda Clark. Jesse Clark consents for Rhoda; no relationship stated. Wit. Gardener Clark. This is consent only. Married by Rev. Eleazer Clay, Baptist. p. 49.

2 October 1777. James COCKE and Lucy Smith. Sur. Obadian Smith. p. 5.

5 September 1777. Charles COGBILL and Lucy Christian. Sur. John Cogbill. p. 5.

24 November 1807. Charles Christian COGBILL and Mary Ann Featherstone, 21 years of age, dau. of Henry Featherstone, Sr. Sur. Henry Walthall, Jr. Wit. Edward Featherstone. Charles Christian son of Charles Cogbill. (Will Book 4, p. 240). Married 26 November by Rev. John Cox, Methodist. p. 88.

31 October 1797. George COGBILL, Jr. and Ridley Chalkley, dau. of David Chalkley who consents. Wit. William Finney. This is consent only. Married 4 November by Rev. Thomas Hardie, Methodist. p. 48.

8 January 1798. Hill COGBILL and Sally Pride. Wit. James Pride and J. A. Pride. This is consent only. Married 3 February by Rev. Needler Robinson, Rector of Dale Parish, Episcopal Church. p. 50.

8 February 1804. Jesse COGBILL and Polly Bass Cogbill, dau. of William Cogbill who consents and is surety. Married by Rev. Needler Robinson, Rector of Dale Parish. Episcopal Church. p.

31 August 1802. John COGBILL and Elizabeth Featherstone, dau. of Henry Featherstone who consents. Sur. David Chockley. Wit. Edward Featherstone. Married 13 September by Rev. Thomas Hardi Methodist. p. 66.

9 July 1789. Thomas COGBILL and Lucy Boisseau. Sur. Daniel Boisseau. Married 19 July by Rev. Needler Robinson, Rector of Dale Parish, Episcopal Church. p. 28.

8 July 1805. Thomas N. COGBILL and Salley Walthall, dau. of Archibald Walthall. Sur. Parke Poindexter. p. 77.

10 December 1790. William COGBILL and Elizabeth Covington, dau of Richard Covington who consents. This is consent only. Married 6 January 1791 by Rev. John Cameron, Rector of Bristol Parish, Episcopal Church. p. 31.

23 March 1796. Charles COLE and Prudence Mann. Married by Rev Nathan Anderson, Methodist. Ministers' Returns p. 385.

10 February 1812. George W. COLE and Caroline M. Wooldridge. Consent of Salley Wooldridge, mother and guardian of Caroline. Sur. Haley Cole. Wit. Martha Branch. p. 112.

2 April 1795. Haley COLE and Salley Morrisett. Married by Rev James Rucks. Ministers' Returns p. 383.

31 May 1784. Hamlin COLE and Sally Bevill, dau. of Biddy Bevil who consents. Sur. William Hill. p. 21.

30 January 1794. John COLE and Rebecca Ellis. Married by Rev. James Rucks. Ministers' Returns p. 381.

21 June 1814. John COLE and Permelia B. Wooldridge, dau. of Salley Wooldridge who consents. Sur. Robert Saunders. Wit. Edward Wooldridge. p. 125.

18 November 1812. Reuben COLE and Elizabeth Fergusson, 21 years of age, dau. of Moses Fergusson, deceased. Sur. William Cole. Married 20 November by Rev. Thomas Anderson. p. 117.

29 December 1795. William COLE and Martha Miles. Married by Rev. Nathan Anderson, Methodist. Ministers' Returns p. 383.

15 November 1800. Joseph COLEMAN and Elizabeth Garrott. Married by Rev. Charles Forsee, Minister of Skinquarter Baptist Church. Ministers' Returns. p. 391.

19 October 1797. Laban COLEMAN and Elizabeth Wormack. Married by Rev. James Rucks. Ministers' Returns p. 384.

25 August 1784. William COLVIN and Maryann Bevill. Sur. John Walke. Wit. James Robertson. p. 21.

9 March 1807. Claiborne CONDRY and Nancy Farmer, dau. of Henry Farmer, deceased. Charles Elam, guardian of Nancy consents for her and is surety. Married 10 March by Rev. Charles Forsee, Skinquarter Baptist Church. p. 85.

4 April 1811. Josiah CONDREY and Sally Robertson, dau. of Jonas Robertson who consents. Sur. Joseph Wilkinson. Wit. S. Wilkinson and F. Robertson. p. 107.

9 July 1810. Norborne B. Cooke and Judith Markham, b. 9 July 1787; dau. of Mary Markham. Sur. George Markham. Wit. J. Bolling. Norborne B. Cooke of Kentucky. p. 103.

29 December 1810. Charles A. COUSINS and Sally R. Stone, dau. of Anna Stone who consents. Sur. Robert Cousins. Wit. James Howlett. Married 1 January 1811 by Rev. John Cox of Petersburg, Methodist. p. 106.

7 July 1810. John COUSINS and Elizabeth Totty, 21 years of age. Sur. Benjamin Totty. Wit. George Cousins. p. 103.

3 December 1773. Peter Cousins and Elizabeth Walthall. Sur. Gerrard Walthall. Wit. Benjamin Watkins. See Peter Cursons. p. 3.

11 January 1799. Richard COUSINS and Ann Robertson. Sur. John Robertson. Wit. William Finney. p. 54.

3 December 1806. Robert COUSINS and Ann Burfoot. Married by Rev. Thomas Lafon, Church of Christ. Ministers' Returns p. 399.

21 December 1797. Thomas COUSINS and Rachel Beavel, dau. of Tamer H. Totty (mother) who consents. Wit. George Cousins and Benjamin Totty. This is consent only. Married by Rev. Thomas Hardie, Methodist, who says Bevill. p. 49.

9 July 1810. William COUSINS and Nancy Mann. Sur. William Dance. p. 103.

22 February 1814. William H. COUSINS and Betsey Franklin, 21 years of age. Sur. Joel Franklin. Married 17 March by Rev. Thomas Lafon, Church of Christ. p. 124.

13 February 1798. John COUZENS and Martha Cozby. Married by Rev. Thomas Hardie, Methodist. These names should be Cousins and Cosby. Ministers' Returns p. 386.

12 November 1807. Lodowick COVINGTON and Salley Randolph, dau. of Mary Whiteford. Sur. William Reames. Both parties over 21. Married 13 Nov. by Rev. John Cox, Methodist. p. 88.

25 December 1783. Thomas COVINGTON and Mary Rowlett. Sur. Edward Eanes. p. 20.

20 March 1810. William COVINGTON and Susannah G. Eanes. Sur. William Eanes. p. 101.

2 December 1815. William COVINGTON and Mary Jefferson Archer, dau. of Field Archer who consents and is surety. Married 3 December by Rev. Joseph Gill, Jr. p. 132.

20 August 1805. Abraham COX and Rhoda Hancock, 21 years of age, dau. of George Hancock, deceased. Sur. Edward Hill. Wit. Obedience Lockett. Married 22 August by Rev. Charles Hopkins. p. 77.

23 January 1787. Edward COX and Martha Friend. Nathaniel Frien consents for Martha. No relationship stated. This is consent only. p. 25.

19 September 1797. Edward COX and Tabitha R. Sherwin. Henry Archer, guardian of Tabitha consents for her. This is consent only. Married 20 September by Rev. Needler Robinson, Rector of Dale Parish, Episcopal Church. p. 48.

___ January 1794. George COX and Mary Friend. Married by Rev. John Cameron, Rector of Bristol Parish, Episcopal Church.

11 November 1805. Henry COX and Mary Traylor, dau. of Archibald Traylor, Sr. who consents. Sur. George Snellings. Married 21 November by Rev. Benjamin Watkins. p. 79.

2 September 1806. Higgerson COX and Elizabeth Cary, dau. of William Cary who consents. Obadiah Cox, guardian of Higgerson, is surety. This name is also spelled Hickerson. Married 4 September by Rev. Benjamin Watkins. P. 82.

27 November 1794. John COX and Mary Rude. Married by Rev. James Rucks. Ministers' Returns p. 382.

9 April 1804. John COX and Susanna S. Cogbill. Married by Rev. Thomas Hardie, Methodist. Ministers' Returns p. 397.

8 August 1797. Obadiah COX and Sarah Ellett, dau. of Cornelius and Hanny Ellett who consent. Sur. William Ellett. Wit. Peter Minor Cary. Married by Rev. Eleazer Clay, Baptist. p. 48.

14 February 1797. William Radford COX and Frances Goodwin, dau. of David Goodwin. Wit. Radford Cox Goodwin and William Goodwin. This is consent only. See William Richard Cox. p. 495.

14 February 1797. William Richard COX and Frances Goodwin. Married by Rev. Nathan Anderson, Methodist. See William Radford Cox. Ministers' Returns p. 385.

5 May 1780. John CRISP and Anne Farmer. Sur. James Turner. p. 11.

13 October 1785. Richard CRITTENDEN and Mary Bowman. Sur. Joseph Taylor. p. 23.

6 January 1800. John CRITTINGTON and Ann Farmer, dau. of Ann Farmer, Senr. who consents. Sur. Joel Cheatham. Wit. Frances Cheatham and John Cary. p. 59.

1801-1802. Edward CROSSTICK and Tabitha Lacy. Married by Rev. Eleazar Clay, Baptist. Ministers' Returns p. 394.

June 1786-June 1789. John CROSTICK and Susannah Pooll (Pool). Married by Rev. Eleazer Clay, Baptist. Ministers' Returns p. 372.

8 November 1813. Abner CRUMP and Amelia Booker, dau. of William Booker, deceased. Sur. Josiah Hobson. p. 122.

9 August 1813. Elias CRUMP and Elizabeth Snellings, 21 years of age, dau. of Sally Snellings. Sur. William Elam. p. 121.

19 April 1815. George CRUMP and Margaret F. Flournoy, 21 years of age, dau. of James Flournoy, deceased. Sur. Jesse Taylor. Wit. Elizabeth Crump. Married 20 April by Rev. Edmund Goode, Baptist. p. 129.

25 January 1779. Gutridge (Goodrich) CRUMP and Judith Howlett.
Sur. John Fore. Wit. Sarah Fore. p. 8.

1 February 1808. John CRUMP and Rhoda Flournoy, dau. of Kezziah
Flournoy. Wit. Gipson Flournoy, Jacob A. Flournoy and Forrest
Flournoy. This is consent only. p. 89.

1 April 1774. Richard CRUMP and Sarah Patterson. Sur. David
Patterson. p. 3.

18 February 1790. Benjamin CULLIN and Rachel Short, dau. of You
Short, who consents. Sur. Daniel Cullin. Married by Rev. James
Smith. p. 30.

13 December 1787. Daniel CULLIN and Elizabeth Shortt, dau. of
Young Shortt who consents. This is consent only. Married 15
December by Rev. William Webber who says Collen and Short. p.
26.

6 April 1799. Richard CUNDIFF and Hannah Gibson. Sur. Jacob
Flournoy. Wit. Nelson Flournoy. Married 9 April by Rev. Benjam
Watkins. p. 55.

13 February 1779. Valentine CUNNINGHAM and Mary Leprade, dau.
of Andrew Leprade whose consent is dated 13 September 1779. Sur
Alexander Cunningham. p. 9.

3 December 1773. Peter CURSONS and Elizabeth Walthall. Sur.
Gerrard Walthall. Wit. Benjamin Watkins. See Peter Cousins.
p. 3.

22 January 1810. John DABNEY and Mary Walthall Hatcher, dau. of
Edward Hatcher, deceased. Consent of A. Bass for Mary. Sur.
William Hatcher. Married 25 January by Rev. Thomas Lafon,
Church of Christ. p. 100.

25 January 1797. Edward DANCE and Saba Burton. Married by Rev.
Needler Robinson, Rector of Dale Parish, Episcopal Church.
Ministers' Returns p. 385.

10 November 1808. Thomas DANCE and Elizabeth Newell, widow of
George Newel; dau. of William Britton, deceased. Sur. Thomas
Britton. p. 93.

11 December 1790. William DANCE and Elizabeth Cousins. Married
by Rev. Needler Robinson, Rector of Dale Parish, Episcopal
Church. Ministers' Returns p. 375.

11 November 1813. William S. DANCE and Lucy Hopson Winfree, dau. of Valentine Winfree, Sr. who consents and is surety. Married 15 November by Rev. Thomas Lafon, Church of Christ. p. 122.

28 March 1815. William DANCE and Sally Irwin, both 21 years of age. Sur. Thomas Cousins. Wit. Mrs. Patsy Gill and William Cousins. Married 30 March by Rev. Joseph Gill. p. 129.

13 July 1812. John W. DANDRIDGE and Lucy M. H. Sharp, dau. of Hayles Sharp, deceased, of Henrico County. Richard Pritchard, step-father of Lucy, consents for her and is surety. p. 114.

12 September 1774. Samuel DAVIES and Amelia Holt. Sur. David Holt. p. 4.

10 February 1799. Edward DAVIS and Nancy Hightower. Edward Davis, Blacksmith and Farier of Richmond. Nancy, housekeeper for James Strange at Buck Hill. James Strange consents for Nancy. p. 54.

_____ 1793. Ezekiel DAVIS and Betsy Puckett. Married by Rev. Eleazer Clay, Baptist. Ministers' Returns p. 381.

10 July 1780. Hezekiah DAVIS and Mary Stiles. Sur. Benjamin Davis. p. 12.

23 January 1786. John DAVIS and Sarah Johnson. Sur. Ephraim Andrews. Wit. Field Traylor. Married 7 February by Rev. William Leigh, Rector of Manchester Parish, Episcopal Church. p. 24.

23 January 1804. John DAVIS and Nancy Roper. Sur. John Roper. p. 70.

_____ 1803. Martin DAVIS and Nancy Moore. Married by Rev. Eleazar Clay, Baptist. Ministers' Returns p. 397.

15 June 1786. Nicholas DAVIS and Sarah Williamson. Married by Rev. John Goode. Ministers' Returns p. 371.

3 August 1772. John DEATON and Martha Rowlett. Sur. Matthew Gibbs. p. 1.

18 December 1811. John DEATON and Polly Patram, widow of Peter Patram. Sur. James Deaton. She was Mary Worsham, dau. of William Worsham. p. 111.

8 July 1798. Stephen DICON and Elizabeth Traylor. Married by
Rev. Thomas Hardie, Methodist. Ministers' Returns p. 388.

11 March 1805. Isham DIER (or Dyer) and Martha Vaden, dau. of
Joseph and Elizabeth Vaden. Sur. William H. Vaden. Wit. Abel
Bowman. p. 75.

22 May 1811. Edward D. DIGGS and Margaret Murchie. Sur. Young
Pankey. p. 108.

22 June 1810. Henry DILLON and Polly S. Cogbill, 21 years of
age. Sur. William Dillon. Married 24 June by Rev. Thomas Lafoi
Church of Christ. p. 103.

7 December 1804. Joseph DILLON and Kittorah Boles Anderson, dav
of Jerusha Anderson, Sr. Sur. William Anderson and Abraham
Holycross. Both 21 years of age. Married 8 Dec. by Rev. Henry
Featherstone, Sr. p. 74.

15 April 1800. Daniel DISHMAN and Mrs. Nany Granger. This is
consent only. p. 60.

June 1788-June 1789. Drury DISHMAN and Anne Eanes. Married by
Rev. Eleazer Clay, Baptist. Ministers' Returns p. 373.

19 January 1793. Drury DISLEMAN and Margaret Totty. Married b
Rev. John Cameron, Rector of Bristol Parish, Episcopal Church.

2 April 1789. Thomas DONNELLY and Elizabeth Cox. This is
consent only. Married 25 April by Rev. James Smith. p. 28.

18 November 1797. Parker DOSS and Angelica Epps Cheatham.
Married by Rev. Nathan Anderson, Methodist. Ministers' Returns
p. 385.

17 August 1801. John DOWNS and Nancy Cunningham, dau. of
Valentine Cunningham who consents. Sur. Philip Webber. Wit.
John Cary. p. 63.

25 October 1809. Theoderick Felix DUDOUIT and Charlotte Jones,
21 years of age, dau. of John Jones, deceased. Sur. William
Jones. p. 98.

6 May 1800. James DUNLAP and Nancy Gilliam Duncan, dau. of
Charles Duncan who consents. Wit. D. Markham. This is consent
only. p. 60.

17 August 1802. Anthony DUNLAVY and Jane Parmer, sister of Polly Hancock who consents. Sur. Thomas Hancock. p. 66.

10 October 1796. William DUNN and Jane Ligon. Sur. William Baugh. William Dunn of Prince George County. Married 20 October by Rev. Needler Robinson, Rector of Dale Parish, Episcopal Church. p. 45.

29 May 1804. William DUNN and Elizabeth Finney. William Mann, guardian of Elizabeth, consents for her. Sur. Henry Walthall. Wit. Z. Martin. p. 72.

18 July 1815. Daniel DUNNAVANT and Mary Blankenship, dau. of Staunton Blankenship. Sur. Edward Goode. Wit. Spencer Woold-ridge and William Finney. Married 19 July by Rev. Edmund Goode, Baptist. p. 130.

3 January 1772. Thomas DUNNAVANT and Winnefred Walthall. Con-sent of Benjamin Walthall, brother of Winnefred, for her. Sur. Philip Dunnavant. Wit. James Walthall and B. Watkins. Name also spelled Dunnivant. p. 1.

22 September 1792. Francis DUNNIVANT and Lydia Flournoy. Sur. Nelson Flournoy. p. 34.

22 October 1780. Josiah DUNNIVANT and Sally Graves, dau. of John Graves. This is consent only. p. 12.

29 January 1806. Ramsey DUNNIVANT and Jensey Elliott Gill, dau. of James Gill who consents. Sur. Parke Poindexter. Wit. V. Winfree, Jr. and William S. Dance. Married by Rev. John Cox, Methodist. p. 80.

1 October 1773. William DURELL and Elizabeth Gross. Sur. William Best. p. 3.

5 November 1801. Burwell DUSEAR and Elizabeth Baugh. Married by Rev. Thomas Hardie, Methodist. Ministers' Returns p. 395.

1 November 1787. Daniel DYSON and Jinny Gill. Married by Rev. John Cameron, Rector of Bristol Parish, Episcopal Church.

15 December 1798. Daniel DYSON and Larkey Rowlett. Married by Rev. Needler Robinson, Rector of Dale Parish, Episcopal Church. Ministers' Returns p. 390.

20 December 1799. Mark DYSON and Nancy Gibbs. Married by Rev. Needler Robinson, Rector of Dale Parish, Episcopal Church. Ministers' Returns p. 390.

1 March 1783. Edward EANES and Frances Rowlett. No surety or witness given. p. 18.

June 1788-June 1789. Ephrim EANES and Aggy Vaden. Married by Rev. Eleazer Clay, Baptist. Ministers' Returns p. 373.

14 May 1782. John EANES and Mary Gill, dau. of Daniel Gill who consents. Sur. Joseph Wells. p. 16.

23 January 1790. John EANES and Margaret Dodd. Married by Rev. John Cameron, Rector of Bristol Parish, Episcopal Church.

14 November 1814. Thomas EANES and Frances Vaden. Sur. William Vaden. Married 17 November by Rev. Joseph Gill, Jr. p. 126.

4 December 1810. William EANES and Elizabeth Britton, dau. of John Britton who consents. Sur. Henry Britton. Married 5 December by Rev. Benjamin Devany. p. 105.

14 January 1802. Buckner EANS and Elizabeth Vaden. Married by Rev. Thomas Hardie, Methodist. Ministers' Returns p. 395.

7 October 1801. Isbane EANS and Elizabeth Belcher. Married by Rev. Thomas Hardie, Methodist. Ministers' Returns p. 395.

_____ 1792. James EANS and Sandil Blankenship. Married b Rev. Eleazer Clay, Baptist. Ministers' Returns p. 380.

12 July 1798. James EANS and Phebe Vaiden. Married by Rev. Thomas Hardie, Methodist. Ministers' Returns p. 388.

22 September 1798. John EANS and Sally Franklin. Married by Rev. Thomas Hardie, Methodist. Ministers' Returns p. 386.

24 June 1774. John EDWARDS and Martha Worsham. William Worsham consents for Martha. No relationship stated. Sur. Thomas Worsham. Wit. Robert Kennon and Elizabeth Loftis. p. 3.

11 November 1811. John Worsham EDWARDS and Wilmoth Gill. Sur. Joseph Gill. Wit. Jacob Gill. p. 110.

10 April 1785. William EDWARDS and Pheby Cogbill. Sur. John Baugh. p. 23.

28 June 1792. William EDWARDS and Polley Britton, dau. of Anderson Britton who consents. This is consent only. Omitted from p. 34. p. 57.

15 October 1793. Benjamin ELAM and Elizabeth Stamford, 21 years of age. Sur. Godfrey Elam. Married 27 October by Rev. George Smith, Baptist, who says Stanford. p. 37.

_____ 1801. Berkeley ELAM and Betsyan Wooldridge. Married by Rev. Charles Forsee, Minister of Skinquarter Baptist Church. Ministers' Returns p. 395.

2 April 1773. Branch ELAM and Dinah Elam. Sur. James Elam. p. 2.

_____ 1801. Branch ELAM and Elizabeth Flournoy. Married by Rev. Charles Forsee, Minister of Skinquarter Baptist Church. Ministers' Returns p. 395.

11 February 1809. Branch ELAM and Mary Snellings, dau. of Alexander Snellings who consents. Sur. John Porter. Wit. Peter Snellings. p. 96.

31 May 1796. Charles ELAM and Phebe Farmer, of lawful age. Sur. John Condrey. Wit. Richard Elam. Married 2 June by Rev. Nathan Anderson, Methodist. p. 44.

10 February 1790. Daniel ELAM, Jr. and Mary Flournoy, dau. of Jacob Flournoy who consents. This is consent only. Married by Rev. Eleazer Clay, Baptist. p. 30.

15 February 1793. Eli ELAM and Betsey Ann Elam, age 21 years, dau. of Marthew Elam. (father or mother?) Sur. John Flournoy. p. 36.

16 March 1785. Gilbert ELAM and Sally Sims. Sur. James Sims. Married by Rev. John Goode. p. 496.

30 November 1808. James ELAM and Elizabeth H. Rudd. Robert Haskins, guardian of Elizabeth, consents for her. Sur. Samuel Flournoy. Wit. Matthew Cheatham. James son of Richard Elam. p. 94.

3 June 1774. John ELAM and Martha Dudley. Sur. George Markham. p. 3.

10 October 1796. John ELAM and Elizabeth McCoy, 21 years of age. Sur. Meredith Childers. Wit. Baxter Folkes. p. 45.

13 January 1812. Joseph ELAM and Caroline Wooldridge. Sur.
William G. Elam. p. 112.

22 March 1795. Peter ELAM and Martha Elam. Married by Rev.
James Rucks. Ministers' Returns p. 383.

29 August 1812. Peter ELAM and Mary Flournoy, dau. of William
Flournoy who consents. Sur. Green Flournoy. p. 115.

21 October 1784. Richard ELAM and Hannah Wooldridge. p. 485.

26 November 1797. Richard ELAM and Winefred Walthall, dau. of
Richard Walthall who consents. Sur. Leonard Cheatham, Jr.
Married 7 December by Rev. Nathan Anderson, Methodist. p. 49.

6 November 1772. Robert ELAM and Elizabeth Gordon. Sur. John
Forsee. p. 2.

29 August 1800. Robert ELAM and Polly Martin. Wit. Thomas N.
Cogbill. This is consent only. Married 10 September by Rev.
Henry Featherstone, Sr. p. 60.

20 November 1803. Robert ELAM and Elizabeth H. Bass, dau. of
Judith Bass who consents. Sur. John W. Bass. p. 69.

13 August 1810. Robert ELAM and Phebe Elam, widow of William
C. Elam. Sur. Robert Baugh. Wit. Claiborn Condray. Married
22 August by Rev. Edmund Goode, Baptist. p. 103.

25 May 1789. Stephen ELAM and Diana Sims. Sur. Edward Sims.
Married by Rev. John Goode who says Dianna. p. 28.

13 March 1794. William Branch ELAM and Michel Cheatham.
Married by Rev. James Rucks. Ministers' Returns p. 382.

26 July 1803. William G. ELAM and Salley Cox, dau. of Henry
Cox who consents. Wit. Thomas Porter. This is consent only.
p. 68.

12 March 1804. William C. ELAM and Jane Waller. Sur. Richard
Elam. p. 71.

10 May 1806. William G. ELAM and Phebe Cheatham. Arthur Akin,
guardian of Phebe, consents for her. Sur. Shadroch Clark. Wit
William Akin and Pleasant Akin. Married 12 May by Rev. Charles
Forsee. p. 81.

26 February 1795. Archibald ELLETT and Tabitha Robertson, dau. of William Robertson who consents. This is consent only. Married 28 February by Rev. James Rucks. p. 40.

30 November 1797. Hezekiah ELLINGTON and Obedience Hatcher. Sur. Armstreat Bruce. Wit. Martha Bruce and Archibald Hatcher. Married by Rev. Thomas Hardie, Methodist. p. 49.

9 February 1785. William ELLIOT and Phebe Rudd, dau. of Thomas Rudd, Jr. who consents. Married 2 March by Rev. John Goode. p. 22.

13 January 1813. Alexander ELLIOTT and Sally Smith, dau. of Benjamin Smith who consents and is surety. Married 14 January by Rev. Thomas Lafon, Church of Christ. p. 118.

22 October 1815. Robert ELLIOTT and Tabitha O. Goode. Sur. William Gates. Wit. Thomas Bass, Jr. p. 131.

1796-1797. Dabney ELLIOTT and Phebe Baugh Walthall. Married by Rev. Eleazer Clay, Baptist. Ministers' Returns p. 383.

26 December 1810. Henry ELLIOTT and Elizabeth Wells, dau. of Michael Wells, Sr. Sur. Dickerson Wells. p. 106.

16 December 1793. John ELLIOTT and Oney Rudd. Sur. Archer Rudd. Wit. Miles C. Finney. p. 38.

22 September 1808. Peter ELLIOTT and Mary Prichard, dau. of Richard Prichard who consents and is surety. p. 92.

23 February 1795. William ELLIOTT and Salley Rudd. Sur. Archer Rudd. Wit. Thomas Finney. p. 40.

10 November 1798. William ELLIOTT and Polly Morrissett, dau. of Jeane Morrissett who consents. Wit. Haley Cole. This is consent only. Married by Rev. Eleazer Clay, Baptist. p. 53.

11 November 1782. William ELLIS and Elizabeth Aiken, dau. of William Akin who consents. Sur. Joseph Aiken. Wit. Arthur Akin. p. 17.

11 February 1799. William ELLYSON and Susanna Elam. Wit. Haley Cole. This is consent only. Married 14 February by Rev. Benjamin Watkins. p. 54.

30 May 1811.   John ENNIS and Mary D. Hare, dau. of John D. Hare
who consents.   Sur. William C. Wells.   John Ennis of Petersburg
p. 109.

21 July 1812.   William EPPES and Eliza Gregory, dau. of Richard
Gregory who consents.   Sur. D. Lipscomb.   p. 115.

12 October 1801.   Joes ESTES and Sally S. Bates, dau. of Eliza
Bates who consents.   Wit. Dutroy Porter and John Friend.   This
is consent only.   Married 13 October by Rev. George Smith,
Baptist.   p. 63.

23 March 1804.   William EVANS and Frances Puckett.   Sur. James
Ferguson.   Wit. Francis Cawley.   Married 24 March by Rev. Henry
Featherstone, Sr.   p. 71.

11 May 1795.   Lewis EVINGTON and Nancy Puller, dau. of Ginney
Puller who consents.   Wit. Samuel Weisiger.   This is consent
only.   p. 41.

26 February 1814.   Robert V. FAGG and Mary Covington, 21 years
of age.   Sur. John A. Pride.   Wit. William Covington.   p. 124.

4 December 1788.   Hayley FARGUS and Ann Williams.   Married by
Rev. Needler Robinson, Rector of Dale Parish, Episcopal Church.
See Haley Fargusson.   p. 374.

25 February 1797.   James FARGUS and Mary Ann Pilkington.   Marri
by Rev. Nathan Anderson, Methodist.   Ministers' Returns p. 385.

23 December 1791.   Littleberry FARGUSS and Nanny Perdue, dau. c
Cleavland Perdue who consents.   This is consent only.   See
Littleberry Furguson.   p. 33.

28 October 1802.   William FARGUSON and Nancy Beasley.   Sur.
Egbert Woodfin.   Married by Rev. Eleazar Clay, Baptist.   p. 66.

13 November 1788.   Haley FARGUSSON and Ann Williams, dau. of
Isaac Williams who consents.   This is consent only.   See Hayley
Fargus.   p. 27.

18 July 1786.   Joseph FARGUSSON and Sally Blankenship.   Sur.
Allen Whitowrth.   p. 24.

17 January 1780.   Thomas FARGUSSON and Martha Newby.   Sur.
Moses Fargusson.   p. 11.

13 June 1779. John FARLEY and Judith Moore Farmer. Isham Farmer consents for Judith; no relationship stated. Sur. Archer Chaulkley. Wit. Colin Ferguson and William Farmer. Bride's name also written Judith Moon Farmer. p. 9.

5 March 1796. John FARLEY and Elizabeth Cheatham, dau. of Elizabeth Cheatham who consents. Sur. Elam Lockett. Married by Rev. Eleazer Clay, Baptist. p. 43.

19 October 1801. Matthew FARLEY and Martha Ashurst, dau. of Robert Ashurst who consents. Wit. William Turpin and Arthur Moseley. This is consent only. Married 22 October by Rev. George Smith, Baptist. p. 64.

3 January 1811. Philip FARLEY and Alice E. Calvin, dau. of William Calvin, Sr. who consents. Sur. Joseph P. Calvin. Married by Rev. John Cox of Petersburg, Methodist. p. 106.

12 September 1810. Abner FARMER and Dorothy Farmer, dau. of Samuel Farmer who consents and is surety. Married by Rev. Thomas Lafon, Church of Christ. p. 104.

24 September 1805. Archer FARMER and Mary Brooks, dau. of Elias Brooks who consents and is surety. Married 26 Sept. by Rev. Thomas Lafon, Church of Christ. p. 78.

20 September 1807. Benjamin FARMER and Nancy Nunnally. Sur. Jeremiah Nunnally. Married by Rev. Edmund Goode, Baptist. p. 87.

10 October 1807. Benjamin FARMER and Susanna Goode. Married by Rev. Charles Forsee, Skinquarter Baptist Church. Ministers' Returns p. 400.

7 February 1778. Forrest FARMER and Ruth Sudberry, dau. of Ezekiel Sudbury who consents. Sur. Daniel Horner. p. 6.

_____ 1790. Henry FARMER and Phebe Sims. Married by Rev. John Goode. Return dated 6 April 1790. Ministers' Returns p. 376.

3 May 1813. Henry FARMER and Elizabeth R. Ware, 21 years of age. Sur. John Turpin. Married 6 May by Rev. Thomas Lafon, Church of Christ. p. 120.

25 January 1780. Hezekiah FARMER and Elizabeth Cheatham. p. 485.

24 January 1810. Horatio FARMER and Patsey Chalkley, dau. of David Chalkley, deceased. Sur. William Beasley. Married by Rev Thomas Lafon, Church of Christ. p. 100.

2 November 1812. Mark FARMER and Nancy Brown, 21 years of age, dau. of John Brown. Sur. Wilson Branch. p. 117.

2 January 1815. Pleasant FARMER and Rebecca Lucadoe, dau. of William Lucadoe who consents. Sur. David Johnson. This name is also spelled Lookado. Married 7 January by Rev. Thomas Lafon, Church of Christ. p. 128.

14 December 1778. Thomas FARMER, Jr. and Lucy Stewart. Sur. William Turner. p. 8.

30 January 1800. Daniel FARQUSSON and Nancy Ferguson, dau. of Judith Ferguson who consents. Sur. Levi Newby. Wit. Page P. Finney. Married by Rev. Eleazer Clay, Baptist. See Daniel Furguson. p. 59.

3 March 1779. George FARRIL and Mary Gibbs, dau. of William Gibbs who consents. Sur. William Tarrel. Wit. William Bell. p. 9.

28 October 1778. Edward FEATHERSTONE and Sarah Ashbrooke. Sur. Peter Ashbrooke. p. 7.

9 April 1781. William FENDLEE and _____ _____. Sur. Peter Franklin. See William Findley. p. 14.

12 February 1810. Asa FERGUSON and Ruth Turner, dau. of William Turner who consents. Sur. Stephen Turner. Married 14 February by Rev. Thomas Lafon, Church of Christ. p. 100.

8 July 1790. Dougald FERGUSON and Elizabeth Archer. Sur. Henry Archer. Wit. Philip Thweatt. p. 31.

6 December 1782. _____ FERGUSSON and Frances Kendell, dau. of Elizabeth Kendall. This is consent only. p. 17.

7 January 1815. Asa FERGUSSON and Prudence Perdue, 21 years of age, dau. of John Perdue. Sur. William Hatchett. See Newby Fergusson. p. 128.

30 May 1811. John FERGUSSON and Betsey Hancock. Sur. Arthur Hancock. Married 8 June by Rev. Benjamin Watkins. p. 109.

18 September 1804. Moses FERGUSSON, Jr. and Frances Graves, dau. of John Graves who consents. Moses Fergusson over 21 years of age. p. 73.

7 January 1815. Newby FERGUSSON and Prudence Perdue. Married by Rev. Thomas Lafon, Church of Christ. See Asa Fergusson. Ministers' Returns p. 410.

9 April 1781. William FINDLEY and _____ _____. Sur. Peter Franklin. See William Fendlee. p. 14.

23 November 1806. Thomas FISHER and Rhoda Hortler. Sur. William Winfree. Married by Rev. Thomas Lafon, Church of Christ who says Fitcher and Hosfler. p. 83.

30 August 1803. William FISHER and Anna Watkins. Sur. David Miller. p. 68.

11 March 1799. Daniel FLOURNOY and Judith Flournoy, dau. of Josiah Flournoy who consents. Wit. Gibson Flournoy. This is consent only. Married by Rev. Eleazer Clay, Baptist. p. 55.

8 January 1787. David FLOURNOY and Elizabeth Britton, dau. of Anderson Britton who consents. This is consent only. p. 25.

9 March 1809. Forrest FLOURNOY and Peggy Crump, dau. of Thomas Crump who consents. Sur. John J. Crump. Wit. John Powell. p. 96.

17 July 1792. Gibson FLOURNOY and Patsy Ashurst. Sur. William Hill. p. 34.

23 March 1811. Green FLOURNOY and Elizabeth Robertson, dau. of James Robertson who consents. Sur. Alexander Moore. Wit. John Porter. p. 107.

3 January 1784. John FLOURNOY and Sally Labarreaire. Sur. John Laprade. p. 20.

1 May 1797. John FLOURNOY and Martha Nunnally. Sur. Edward Nunnally. Married 4 May by Rev. Benjamin Watkins. p. 47.

23 January 1811. John FLOURNOY and Wealthy Ann Brummal. 21 years of age. Sur. Daniel Furquren. p. 106.

15 May 1812. Joseph FLOURNOY and Polly Jennings. Sur. John W. Jennings. Wit. Nancy Flournoy and Edward Bass. Joseph son of William Flournoy, Jr. 1. 114.

10 March 1812. Josiah FLOURNOY and Elizabeth Green Cheatham. Sur. Samuel Flournoy.

6 December 1814. Mark F. FLOURNOY and Edith F. Walthall, dau. of Richard Walthall, deceased. Robert Baugh, guardian of Edith consents for her. Sur. Francis W. Dunnivant. Wit. Richard Elam. Married by Rev. Edmund Goode. p. 126.

1801-1802. Nelson FLOURNOY and Elizabeth Taylor. Married by Rev. Eleazar Clay, Baptist. Ministers' Returns p. 394.

11 December 1795. Obadiah FLOURNOY and Jenny Flournoy. Josiah Flournoy, father of Obadiah, consents for him. Wit. Daniel Flournoy. This is consent only. Married 17 December by Rev. Benjamin Watkins. p. 42.

24 March 1798. Obadiah FLOURNOY and Nancy Gibson. Married by Rev. Benjamin Watkins. Ministers' Returns p. 387.

13 August 1804. Samuel FLOURNOY and Phebe Walthall, dau. of Richard Elam who consents. Wit. Parke Poindexter and Betsey G. Elam. Could this mean step-daughter? p. 72.

9 November 1812. Seth Ward FLOURNOY and Margaret Hill Rudd, 21 years of age. Sur. Robert Rudd. p. 117.

24 December 1806. Thomas FLOURNOY and Jane Robertson, dau. of James Robertson who consents. Sur. Alexander Moore. Wit. John Porter. Married 25 December by Rev. Charles Forsee, Skinquarter Baptist Church. p. 84.

21 December 1790. William FLOURNOY and Phebe Farmer. Sur. Jack Flournoy. Married 24 December by Rev. Benjamin Watkins. p. 31

3 April 1772. William FOLKS and Catharine Knibb. Sur. Edward Worsham. p. 1.

31 March 1783. David FORD and Ann Goode, dau. of John Goode who consents. This is consent only. p. 18.

25 May 1813. Enock FORD and Ann Dodson, dau. of William and Mary Dodson who consent. Sur. B. Andrews. p. 120.

5 September 1805. Thomas FORE and Paulina F. Branch. Married by Rev. Thomas Anderson. Ministers' Returns p. 398.

23 January 1793. Peter FORQUERON and Caty Farmer. Married by Rev. Needler Robinson, Rector of Dale Parish, Episcopal Church. Ministers' Returns p. 377.

15 February 1813. Nathaniel FORRESTER and Elizabeth Alphin, both 21 years of age. Sur. William Baldwin. p. 119.

26 April 1796. Charles FORSEE and Nancy Robertson. Sur. William Bass. Wit. Archibald Bass. Married 30 April by Rev. James Rucks. p. 44.

19 November 1804. William FORSEE and Phebe Bass, dau. of Edward Bass. Sur. Edmund Purdie. Married by Rev. Benjamin Watkins. p. 74.

9 December 1792. James FOUNTAIN and Rebecca Bass. Dan W. Collum, guardian of Rebecca consents for her. This is consent only. p. 35.

_____ _____ 1792. _____ FOWLER and Patience P_____. Married by Rev. Eleazer Clay, Baptist. Manuscript mutilated. Ministers' Returns p. 380.

4 June 1788. Bernard FOWLER and Temperance Pankey, dau. of Stephen Pankey, Jr. who consents. This is consent only. p. 27.

1796-1797. Gardner FOWLER and Sarah Davis. Married by Rev. Eleazer Clay, Baptist. Ministers' Returns p. 386.

15 October 1805. Jeremiah FOWLER and Elizabeth Puckett, dau. of Nathaniel Puckett. Sur. Archer Puckett. p. 78.

25 December 1798. John FOWLER and Sarah Patram. Married by Rev. Nathan Anderson, Methodist. Ministers' Returns p. 388.

18 January 1798. Joshua FOWLER and Patience Blankenship. Married by Rev. Thomas Hardie, Methodist. Ministers' Returns p. 386.

8 February 1814. King F. FOWLER and Salley Morris, 21 years of age. Sur. Benjamin Puckett. Married 12 February by Rev. Thomas Anderson, Sr. p. 124.

_____ _____ 1793. Pleasant FOWLER and Priscilla Berry. Married by Rev. Eleazer Clay, Baptist. Ministers' Returns p. 381.

June 1788-June 1789. Thomas FOWLER and Sarah Traylor. Married by Rev. Eleazer Clay, Baptist. Ministers' Returns p. 373.

13 March 1785. William FOWLER and Judith Sallee', dau. of Abram Sallee' who consents. This is consent only. p. 22.

1 March 1796. William FOWLER and Susanna Saunders. Susanna signs her own consent. This is consent only. p. 43.

1796-1797. William FOWLER and Phebe Patram. Married by Eleazer Clay, Baptist. Ministers' Returns p. 386.

June 1787-June 1788. Zebulon FOWLER and Ann Traylor. Married by Rev. Eleazer Clay, Baptist. Ministers' Returns p. 372.

13 December 1808. James FOWLKES and Prudence Cheatham, 21 years of age, dau. of Josiah Cheatham, deceased. Sur. John Cheatham. p. 94.

11 December 1806. Archer FRANKLIN and Nancy Belcher. Married by Rev. Thomas Lafon, Church of Christ. Ministers' Returns p. 399.

11 January 1779. David FRANKLIN and (illegible). Sur. Valentin Ball. p. 8.

15 December 1802. James FRANKLIN and Elizabeth Cousins. Married by Rev. Henry Featherstons, Sr. Ministers' Returns p. 396.

24 September 1789. Joel FRANKLIN and Susanna Brintle. Married by Rev. Richard Garrettson of the town of Petersburg. Ministers Returns p. 376.

2 March 1801. John FRANKLIN and Nancy Eanes, dau. of William Eanes, Senr. who consents. This is consent only. Married 12 March by Rev. Thomas Hardie, Methodist. p. 62.

25 December 1798. Owen FRANKLIN and Elizabeth Roper, dau. of Joseph Roper who consents. Wit. James Burnett. This is consent only. Married 27 December by Rev. Benjamin Watkins. p. 54.

25 September 1799. Thomas FRANKLIN and Oney Chappell. Married by Rev. Thomas Hardie, Methodist. Ministers' Returns p. 389.

12 March 1788. Alexander FRANKLYN and Anne Hoy. Married by Rev. John Cameron, Rector of Bristol Parish, Episcopal Church.

11 November 1791. Jesse FRANKLYN and Elizabeth Irwin, dau. of Thomas Irwin who consents. This is consent only. Married 18 November by Rev. Richard Garrettson of Petersburg. p. 33.

25 March 1780. Josiah FRANKLYN and Mary Hocks. Sur. Richard Burton. p. 11.

24 December 1806. Simon FRASER and Margaret Smith, 21 years of age, dau. of Richard Smith. Sur. Thomas Blankenship. Married 25 December by Rev. Henry Featherstone, Sr. p. 84.

8 February 1813. Thomas FREEMAN and Rebecca Lively. Sur. Thomas Watkins, Jr. Married 18 February. Married by Rev. Andrew Syme, Rector of Episcopal Church in Petersburg. p. 118.

9 June 1802. John FRIEND and Susan Ball, dau. of Capt. William Ball. Wit. Daniel Ball. p. 65.

7 March 1776. Joseph FRIEND and Elizabeth Bass. Sur. John Osborne. P. 5.

27 August 1798. Joseph FRIEND and Amelia Taylor Sherwin. Consent of Henry Archer. (For which one?) This is consent only. p. 52.

1 February 1802. Capt. William FRIEND and Ann Patterson, dau. of David Patterson who consents. Married by Rev. Needler Robinson, Rector of Dale Parish. Episcopal Church. p. 65.

20 March 1798. Drury FRITH and Polley Martin, dau. of Thomas Martin who consents. Sur. William Frith. Wit. John Markham, Jr. Married by Rev. Nathan Anderson, Methodist, who says Drewry. p. 51.

_____ 1792. William FRITH and Annis Hill. Married by Rev. Eleazer Clay, Baptist. See William Fryth. Ministers' Returns p. 380.

19 March 1798. William FRITH and Tabitha Keen. Sur. Drury Frith. Wit. John Markham, Jr. Married by Rev. Nathan Anderson, Methodist. p. 51.

6 April 1781. Joshua FROST and ____ ____. Sur. John Pride. p. 14.

24 December 1791. William FRYTH and Annie Hill, dau. of Ann Hill who consents. Wit. Field Traylor. This is consent only. See William Frith. p. 33.

11 December 1797. Irby FUQUA and Betty Horner, dau. of Daniel Horner who consents. This is consent only. Married 21 December by Rev. Thomas Hardie, Methodist. p. 49.

25 August 1812. Irby FUQUA and Nancy Stewart, 21 years of age, dau. of Patsey Stewart. Sur. William Fuqua. Married by Rev. Thomas Lafon, Church of Christ. p. 116.

10 October 1804. John FUQUA and Lucy Clayton. Hezekiah Horner, guardian of Lucy, consents for her and is surety. p. 73.

27 February 1811. Samuel FUQUA and Elizabeth Robertson, dau. of George Robertson, deceased. Sur. Leonard Nunnally. p. 107.

30 January 1800. Daniel FURGUSON and Nancy Furquren. Married by Rev. Eleazar Clay, Baptist. See Daniel Farqusson. Ministers Returns p. 393.

1801-1802. Darius FURGUSON and Martha Clarke. Married by Rev. Eleazar Clay, Baptist. Ministers' Returns p. 394.

June 1787-June 1788. King FURGUSON and Fanny Vaden. Married by Rev. Eleazer Clay, Baptist. Ministers' Returns p. 372.

_____ 1791. Littleberry FURGUSON and Nanny Perdue. Married by Rev. Eleazer Clay. Returned in a list dated 1792. See Littleberry Farguss.. Ministers' Returns p. 380.

June 1788-June 1789. Robert FURGUSON and Elizabeth Hubbard. Married by Rev. Eleazer Clay, Baptist. Ministers' Returns p. 373.

_____ 1792. Bartlet FURQUREN and Faney Woodcock. Married by Rev. Eleazer Clay, Baptist. Ministers' Returns p. 379.

1797-1798. James FURQUREN and Mary Farmer. Married by Rev. Eleazer Clay, Baptist. Ministers' Returns p. 387.

1797-1799. Samuel FURQUREN and Mary Newby. Married by Rev. Eleazer Clay, Baptist. Ministers' Returns p. 392.

1 March 1805. John GAMBLE and Charlotte Smith Duncan, not of age, dau. of Charles Duncan who consents. Sur. William H. Cabell. p. 75.

22 May 1791. Henry GARDNER and Phebe Sudberry. Married by Rev. Needler Robinson, Rector of Dale Parish, Episcopal Church. Ministers' Returns p. 375.

3 January 1795. Thomas GARDNER and Ann Horner, 21 years of age. Writes her own consent. Dau. of Daniel Horner. Wit. Henry Winfree. This is consent only. p. 40.

7 December 1778. John GARROTT and Elizabeth Ammonett. Sur. Elisha Wooldridge. Elizabeth was dau. of Andrew and Jean (Morriset) Ammonet and grand dau. of Jacob Ammonet. John Garrott was son of Isaac Garrott of Dale Parish. Will 6 Feb. 1775 names son John Chesterfield. Will Book II, p. 275. p. 7.

6 June 1799. David GARY and Elizabeth Carter. Married by Rev. Needler Robinson, Rector of Dale Parish, Episcopal Church. Ministers' Returns p. 390.

4 November 1805. Thomas E. GRAY and Rebecca H. Boisseau, dau. of Daniel Boisseau who consents. Sur. John B. Read. Wit. Patrick Boisseau. p. 79.

18 December 1805. William GARY and Dolley Farmer, 21 years of age, dau. of Thomas Farner. Sur. John McLelland. p. 79.

GATES: SEE GATTS

15 May 1786. Alexander GATES and Mary Boles. Married by Rev. John Goode. Ministers' Returns p. 371.

31 May 1804. Eppes GATES and Patience Robertson, dau. of James Robertson who consents. Sur. Josiah Stewart. p. 72.

22 June 1781. James GATES and Sarah Bass, dau. of Thomas Bass, Sr. Sur. Blanks Moody. Wit. Edward Bass. Married 28 June by Rev. William Hickman. p. 14.

17 May 1796. James GATES and Sarah Ashbrook. Sur. Daniel Ashbrook. Married 21 May by Rev. Benjamin Watkins. p. 44.

6 November 1809. James GATES, Jr. and Judith Forsee, dau. of Rev. Charles Forsee. Sur. William Goode. Wit. Tapley Goode. James son of James Gates, Sr. p. 98.

11 April 1786. John GATES and Rhoda Boles. Married by Rev. John Goode. Ministers' Returns p. 371.

27 January 1791. Joseph GATES and Polly Boles. Sur. Henry Farmer. Married by Rev. Walthall Robertson, Baptist. Return dated 14 November. p. 32.

20 October 1783. Ricahrd GATES and _____ _____. Sur. Jere Nunnally. p. 19.

26 May 1809. Temple GATES and Phoebe Eanes Granger, dau. of Aaron Granger who consents. Sur. Daniel Dishman. p. 97.

22 April 1801. William GATES, Jr. and Mary Howell. Wit. James Parker. Signed their own consent. This is consent only. See William Gatts. p. 62.

13 May 1802. William GATES and Polly W. Cheatham, dau. of Phebe Cheatham who consents. Sur. Francis Walthall. See William Gatts. p. 65.

14 March 1800. Jacob GATTS and Susanna Gatts. Married by Rev. Charles Forsee, Minister of Skinquarter Baptist Church. Ministers' Returns p. 391.

23 April 1801. William GATTS and Mary Howell. Married by Rev. Charles Forsee, Minister of Skinquarter Baptist Church. See William Gates. Ministers' Returns p. 395.

13 May 1802. William GATTS and Polley Cheatham. Married by Rev. Charles Forsee, Minister of Skinquarter Baptist Church. See William Gates. Ministers' Returns p. 393.

10 December 1810. Alexander GIBBS and Jane Dyson, dau. of Daniel Dyson who consents and is surety. Married 20 December by Rev. John Cox of Petersburg, Methodist. p. 105.

21 Deceber 1802. Francis GIBBS and Nancy Davis, 21 years of age. William Gibbs, father of Francis, consents for him. This is consent only. p. 66.

21 February 1787. John GIBBS and Martha Baugh. Wit. Alexander Baugh and John Pride. This is consent only. p. 25.

6 July 1793. John Gibbs and Mary Gill. Married by Rev. John Cameron, Rector of Bristol Parish, Episcopal Church.

18 March 1786. Matthew GIBBS and Betty Davis. Married by Rev. William Leigh, Rector of Manchester Parish, Episcopal Church. Ministers' Returns p. 370.

_____ 1792. Peter GIBBS and Elizabeth Patram. Married by Rev. Eleazer Clay, Baptist. Ministers' Returns p. 379.

8 March 1815. Peter D. GIBBS and Elizabeth Gill, dau. of William Gill who consents. Sur. Peter Gill. Wit. William Varnier. Married 11 March by Rev. Joseph Gill, Jr. p. 129.

13 May 1785. William GIBBS and Anne Patram. Sur. Miles Worsham. p. 23.

15 April 1790. Aaron GILL and Jency Gill. Married by Rev. John Cameron, Rector of Bristol Parish, Episcopal Church.

23 March 1813. Benjamin GILL and Polly Ann Bennett, 21 years of age. Sur. Eli Bennett. Married by Rev. Henry Bridgewater. p. 119.

26 January 1778. Daniel GILL and Mary Dyson (Dison). Francis Dison consents for Mary. No relationship stated. Sur. John Gill. p. 6.

3 December 1811. Daniel GILL and Salley Royall, 21 years of age, dau. of Francis Gill. Sur. William Gill. Married 12 December by Rev. Joseph Gill. p. 111.

18 February 1786. Edward GILL and Ann Eanes. Married by Rev. William Leigh, Rector of Manchester Parish, Episcopal Church. Ministers' Returns p. 370.

13 February 1804. Goode GILL and Sally Smith, dau. of John Smith who consents and is surety. p. 71.

9 April 1804. Hubbard GILL and Elizabeth Allen. Married by Rev. Thomas Hardie, Methodist. Ministers' Returns p. 397.

1801-1802. Jacob GILL and Polley Akin. Married by Rev. Eleazar Clay, Baptist. Ministers' Returns p. 394.

30 November 1809. James GILL and Martha Brown, dau. of Samuel Brown, deceased. Sur. Robert Partin. Wit. Alexander Brown. p. 99.

_____ 1803. Jesse GILL and Frances Baugh. Married by Rev. Eleazar Clay, Baptist. Ministers' Returns p. 397.

_____ 1790. John GILL and Bidy Clark. Married by Rev. John Goode. Return dated 6 April 1790. Ministers' Returns p. 376.

10 November 1803. John GILL and Martha Irwin, dau. of Thomas Irwin who consents. Married by Rev. Needler Robinson, Rector of Dale Parish, Episcopal Church. p. 69.

15 November 1788. Joseph GILL and Mary Brown. Married by Rev. John Cameron, Rector of Bristol Parish, Episcopal Church.

4 December 1788. Joseph GILL and Fanny Glassco. Married by Rev. John Cameron, Rector of Bristol Parish. Episcopal Church.

4 April 1810. Joseph GILL and Judith Henry. Sur. John Smith.
p. 101.

25 December 1788. Nader GILL and Elizabeth Granger. Married by
Rev. John Cameron, Rector of Bristol Parish, Episcopal Church.

19 May 1800. Robert GILL and Elizabeth Rowlett, of lawful age,
dau. of William Rowlett who consents. Wit. John Mann and John
Rowlett. This is consent only. Married 29 May by Rev. Needler
Robinson, Rector of Dale Parish, Episcopal Church. p. 60.

28 April 1786. Stephen GILL and Betsy Bolton. Married by Rev.
William Leigh, Rector of Manchester Parish. Episcopal Church.
Ministers' Returns p. 370.

4 April 1814. Thomas GILL and Susanna Gill, both 21 years of
age. Dau. of William Gill. Sur. William Berry. Married 7
April by Rev. Joseph Gill, Jr. p. 125.

9 November 1795. Vaden GILL and Martha Moore. Sur. Wilson
Vaden. Married 24 November by Rev. Nathan Anderson, Methodist.
p. 42.

31 January 1809. Vaden GILL and Patsey Willson, 21 years of
age, dau. of Drury Willson. Sur. George Willson. p. 95.

7 February 1790. William GILL and Anne Andress. Married by
Rev. John Cameron, Rector of Bristol Parish, Episcopal Church.

30 September 1811. William GILL and Frances Rowlett Eanes,
dau. of Edward Eanes who consents. Sur. Joseph Gill. Married
3 October by Rev. Joseph Gill. p. 110.

12 February 1810. _____ GILLIAM and Frances Patterson, dau. of
Joel Patterson who consents. This is consent only. p. 100.

15 December 1810. Alban GILPIN and Virginia Ann Moseley, dau.
of Edward Moseley. Sur. Allan McRae. Wit. Wager S. Moseley.
p. 106.

16 July 1814. Abraham C. GODSEY and Polly Howard. Peter Porter
consents for Polly. No relationship stated. Sur. Solomon
Godsey. Wit. Dorothea R. Porter. p. 125.

__ August 1791. Henry GODSEY and Polly Chappell, dau. of Ann
Chappell who consents. This is consent only. p. 32.

24 February 1814. John GODSEY and Polley Moore, dau. of William D. Moore who consents. Sur. Alexander Moore. p. 124.

20 October 1808. Solomon GODSEY and Phebe Hancock. Sur. Zelphr. McGruder. Married 22 October by Rev. Benjamin Watkins. p. 93.

1 March 1800. Thomas GODSEY and Phebe Baugh Elam, dau. of Branch Elam who consents. Sur. Berkeley Elam. Wit. Francis Cheatham. Married 6 March by Rev. Charles Forsee, Minister of Skinquarter Baptist Church who says Phebe Branch Elam. p. 60.

21 November 1781. William GODSEY and Biddy Hall. Sur. Edward Hall. p. 15.

8 December 1790. Benjamin GOODE and Martha Robertson. Sur. Stephan Elam. Married by Rev. Walthall Robertson, Baptist. p. 31.

17 May 1802. Edmund Goode and Patience M. Rucks, dau. of James Rucks who consents. Sur. John Goode. Married 19 May by Rev. Charles Forsee, Minister of the Skinquarter Baptist Church. p. 65.

29 January 1813. Edward GOODE and Synthia Akin, dau. of Thomas Akin who consents. Sur. Robert Royall. Married 1 February by Rev. Thomas Lafon, Church of Christ. p. 118.

16 December 1797. Jesse GOODE and Sally Cogbill, dau. of Lucy Cogbill who consents. Wit. Edward Goode and Henry Walthall. This is consent only. Married 25 December by Rev. Thomas Hardie, Methodist. p. 49.

_____ 1792. John GOODE and Molley Bland. Married by Rev. Eleazer Clay, Baptist. Ministers' Returns p. 380.

3 March 1796. John GOODE and Martha Cheatham. Married by Rev. Nathan Anderson, Methodist. Ministers' Returns p. 385.

10 October 1803. John GOODE and Disey Cleatin. Married by Rev. Henry Featherstone, Sr. Ministers' Returns p. 396.

9 November 1811. John GOODE and Elizabeth Anders, 21 years of age. Wit. Richard Smith and David Johnson. This is consent only. p. 110.

1785-1786. Robert GOODE and Ann Cheatham. Married by Rev. Eleazer Clay, Baptist. Ministers' Returns p. 371.

2 October 1806. Robert GOODE and Mary Watkins, dau. of Mary
Watkins who consents. Sur. F. Watkins. Wit. Martha Watkins.
Married 9 October by Rev. Charles Forsee, Minister of Skinquarter
Baptist Church. p. 83.

6 November 1809. Tapley GOODE and Tabitha Cheatham, dau. of
Isham Cheatham, deceased. Charles Forsee, guardian of Tabitha
consents for her. Sur. William Goode. Married 9 Nov. by Rev.
Charles Forsee, Skinquarter Baptist Church who says Tabitha O.
Cheatham. p. 98.

June 1788-June 1789. William GOODE and Phebe Bass. Married by
Rev. Eleazer Clay, Baptist. Ministers' Returns p. 373.

27 May 1780. Collins GOODING, Jr. and Susanna Chappel. Sur.
Collins Gooding, Sr. p. 12.

6 October 1802. John B. GOODRICH and Rebecca Pearce. Married
by Rev. Needler Robinson, Rector of Dale Parish, Episcopal
Church. Ministers' Returns p. 391.

14 May 1801. William GOODWIN and Mary Archer. Married by Rev.
Thomas Hardie, Methodist. Ministers' Returns p. 395.

23 June 1778. Daniel GORDON and Charlotte Quarles. Sur.
Solomon Gordon. p. 6.

8 August 1793. Francis GORDON and Mary Nunnally. Sur. Hopkins
Moore. p. 37.

June 1786-June 1787. Julius GORDON and Elizabeth Traylor.
Married by Rev. Eleazer Clay, Baptist. Ministers' Returns p.
372.

12 October 1772. Solomon GORDON and Barbara Baker, dau. of
Thomas Baker. Sur. William Baker. p. 2.

29 August 1781. William GORDON and Sally Elam. Sur. William
Elam. p. 14.

15 December 1801. Joseph GRAMMAR and Rebecca Worsham, dau. of
Sarah Worsham who consents. Wit. William Burton. This is
consent only. Married 24 December by Rev. Henry Featherstone,
Sr., who says Gramer. p. 64.

24 November 1806. Burrell GRAMMER and Martha Worsham, 21 years
of age. Sur. William Burton. p. 83.

1 August 1799. Aaron GRANGER and Polly Dodd. Married by Rev.
Thomas Hardie, Methodist. Ministers' Returns p. 389.

June 1787-June 1788. John GRANT and Elizabeth Franklin.
Married by Rev. Eleazer Clay, Baptist. Ministers' Returns p.
372.

5 May 1784. Armistead GRAVES and Mary Ann Atchison. Sur. John
Graves. p. 21.

1797-1799. Arthur GRAVES and Elizabeth Clark. Married by Rev.
Eleazer Clay, Baptist. Ministers' Returns p. 392.

1797-1798. Benjamin GRAVES and Polley Hill. Married by Rev.
Eleazer Clay, Baptist. Ministers' Returns p. 387.

25 December 1811. Benjamin G. GRAVES and Milly F. Hancock.
William Hancock, brother of Milly, consents for her and is surety.
Benjamin G. Graves of Nottoway County. p. 111.

12 February 1791. Charles GRAVES and Dorcas Clay. Married by
Rev. Needler Robinson, Rector of Dale Parish, Episcopal Church.
Ministers' Returns p. 375.

1797-1799. Isham GRAVES and Ellinor Perdue. Married by Rev.
Eleazer Clay, Baptist. Ministers' Returns p. 392.

1796-1797. John GRAVES and Salley Wilkinson. Married by Rev.
Eleazer Clay, Baptist. Ministers' Returns p. 386.

14 March 1814. Matthew GRAVES and Martha Bruce, dau. of Armstreat
Bruce who consents. Sur. Leroy Branch. p. 124.

4 November 1815. James GRAY and Harriet Anna Wherry, dau. of
Jesse Wherry. Sur. James Caskill. p. 131.

28 November 1805. Stephen W. GRAY and Eliza Carter, 21 years of
age. Sur. Richard Hughes. p. 79.

6 January 1802. William GRAY and Winifred Newby. Sur. James
Clarke, Wit. Robert Fargusson and John Russell. Married by
Rev. Eleazar Clay, Baptist. p. 64.

12 October 1807. David GREENHILL and Eliza C. Hudson, dau. of
Lewellin Hudson who consents. Sur. Richard C. Hudson. David
Greenhill of Charlotte County. p. 87.

17 January 1782. Joseph GREENHOWE and Elizabeth Breade. Sur.
John Windlee (or Wyndle). p. 16.

26 June 1805. Fendall GREGORY and Mary Gregory, dau. of Richard
Gregory. Sur. John Pegram, Jr. Wit. Peter Franklin. p. 77.

1801-1802. John GREGORY and Polly FURGUSON. Married by Rev. Eleazar Clay, Baptist. Ministers' Returns p. 394.

24 December 1789. Thomas GREGORY and Elizabeth Baker, dau. of John Baker, Sr. who consents. This is consent only. Married by Rev. Eleazer Clay, Baptist. p. 29.

16 May 1778. George GRIFFIS and Milly Byrd. Sur. William Shaw p. 6.

16 January 1785. Haley GRISEL and Betsy Langsdon. Married by Rev. Eleazer Clay, Baptist. Ministers' Returns p. 369.

8 August 1808. Bolling B. HALL and Frances Blankenship, 21 yea of age, dau. of Olive Blankenship. Sur. Jacob Brintle, Sr. P. 92.

4 July 1809. James HALL and Polly Brintle, 21 years of age. Dau. of Jacob Brintle, Sr. who consents. Sur. Edward Nunnally. p. 97.

9 July 1803. John HALL and Dolly Burton, dau. of Sarah Burton who consents. Sur. Richard Burton. Wit. William Dance. Married 14 July by Rev. Needler Robinson, Rector of Dale Parish Episcopal Church. p. 67.

23 December 1814. Lee Roy HALL and Phebe Rowlett, dau. of Pete Rowlett who consents. Sur. John Rowlett. p. 127.

7 August 1775. William HALL and Dorothy Young. Sur. David Holt. p. 4.

28 April 1789. William Williamson HALL and Obedience T. Branch dau. of Lucy Branch who consents. Sur. William Bottoms. Wit. John L. Cooper. p. 27.

1 September 1796. William HAMBLING and Martha Goode. Married by Rev. Thomas Hardie, Methodist. Ministers' Returns p. 383.

26 August 1778. Charles HAMLIN and Martha Nunnally. Sur. John Hill. p. 7.

4 February 1788. Arthur HANCOCK and Sally Cox. Married by Eleazar Clay, Baptist. p. 485.

10 September 1783. Bennett HANCOCK and Mary Bryan. Sur. John Hicks, Jr. Wit. George Markham. p. 19.

20 September 1789. Francis HANCOCK and Elizabeth Cox, dau. of Higgason Cox who consents. Wit. Arthur Hancock. This is consent only. Married 8 October by Rev. James Smith. p. 28.

10 April 1786. George HANCOCK and Obedience Newby. Married by Rev. William Leigh, Rector of Manchester Parish, Episcopal Church. Ministers' Returns p. 370.

3 March 1803. Green HANCOCK and Janey Martin. Married by Rev. Benjamin Watkins. Ministers' Returns p. 396.

17 September 1801. Henry HANCOCK and Nancy Gipson. Married by Rev. Benjamin Watkins. Ministers' Returns p. 393.

1 March 1813. Jeremiah HANCOCK and Elizabeth Pankey. Sur. Samuel Hancock. p. 119.

9 November 1812. Newby HANCOCK and Margaret Gregory, dau. of Thomas Gregory who consents. Sur. Archer Chalkley. p. 117.

22 October 1778. Simon HANCOCK and Mary Cheatham. Sur. George Markham. p. 7.

12 January 1801. Thomas HANCOCK and Polly Parmer or Farmer. Wit. Phebe Pool. This is consent only. p. 62.

11 February 1772. William HANCOCK and Ann Hill. Sur. Richard Elam. Wit. Stephen Pankey, Jr. p. 1.

8 February 1791. Henry HANSON and Ruth Stiles. This is consent only. Married 26 February by Rev. Needler Robinson, Rector of Dale Parish, Episcopal Church. p. 32.

27 October 1791. Thomas HARDIE and Sarah Featherstone. Henry Featherstone consents for Sarah; no relationship stated. Sur. William Featherstone. p. 33.

7 May 1775. William HARDIMAN, Jr. and Ann Dent Black, dau. of William Black. Sur. Archibald Blair. Wit. Ann Blair. William Hardiman, Jr. of Charles City County. p. 4.

9 January 1809. Robert HARDING and Sally Hancock, dau. of George Hancock who consents and is surety. Married by Rev. Eleazar Clay, Baptist. p. 95.

19 December 1780. William HARDING and Susanna Totty. No surety. p. 13.

12 November 1810. John HAREL and Elizabeth Pearce. Sur.
Patrick Kelley. Married 22 November by Rev. Jordan Martin.
p. 105.

16 February 1779. John HARRIS and Elizabeth Branch, dau. of
Samuel Branch who consents and is surety. p. 9.

20 May 1794. Capt. John HARRIS, Jr. and Rebecca Britton, dau.
of Anderson Britton who consents. Sur. John Saunders. Wit.
Francis Goode. p. 38.

17 February 1803. Nathaniel HARRIS and Elizabeth Leigh.
Married by Rev. Needler Robinson, Rector of Dale Parish,
Episcopal Church. Ministers' Returns p. 391.

_____ 1791. Richardson HARRIS and Polley Bryars. Marrie
by Rev. James Smith. Return dated 10 March 1791, Manakin Town.
Ministers' Returns p. 377.

1 September 1786. Thomas HARRIS and Polly Carter, dau. of John
Carter who consents. This is consent only. Married 7 Septembe
by Rev. William Webber, Baptist. p. 24.

10 April 1809. Benjamin Munford HARRISON and Ann P. Atkinson,
dau. of Roger Atkinson who consents. Sur. John Allison. Wit.
Thomas Jones. p. 96.

22 January 1788. Cuthbert HARRISON and Frances Holt, dau. of
Betty Holt who consents. Wit. Thomas Holt. This is consent
only. Married 30 January by Rev. John Cameron, Rector of
Bristol Parish, Episcopal Church. p. 26.

8 August 1799. Richard HARRISON and Sarah Chalkley. Married b
Rev. Thomas Hardie, Methodist. Ministers' Returns p. 389.

3 August 1813. William HARRISON and Louisa Alice Goode, dau. o
Alice Goode who consents. Sur. Francis Goode. p. 121.

15 September 1802. Armstead HARVILL and Beedy Hobbs. Sur.
Isaac Donaldson. Wit. Adam Lee and Nacy Lee. p. 66.

25 February 1786. John HASE and Anne Burton. Married by Rev.
John Cameron, Rector of Bristol Parish, Episcopal Church.

3 August 1813. Maj. Aaron Haskins and Elizabeth D. Hunley.
Sur. Thomas Burfoot, Sr. Wit. Jordan Martin and Richard W.
Bass. p. 121.

20 November 1797. Robert HASKINS and Mary P. Hill, dau. of John Hill who consents. This is consent only. Married 25 November by Rev. George Smith, Baptist. p. 49.

9 September 1811. Robert HASKINS and Keziah Hancock, dau. of Anenias Hancock who consents. Sur. Samuel Wooddy. p. 109.

4 December 1811. Abner HATCHER and Polly Fergusson, 21 years of age. Dau. of William Fergusson. Sur. Obed Hatcher. p. 111.

27 April 1799. Archibald HATCHER and Anna Boisseau. Married by Rev. Thomas Hardie, Methodist. Ministers' Returns p. 389.

22 December 1798. Benjamin HATCHER and Susanna Boisseau. Sur. Patrick Boisseau. Wit. Anner Boisseau. p. 54.

14 June 1808. Benjamin HATCHER and Elizabeth W. Fowler. Isaac Sallee, guardian of Elizabeth, consents for her. This is consent only. p. 91.

23 May 1811. Charles R. HATCHER and Barbara Hancock. Sur. William Hancock. p. 108.

4 February 1792. Daniel HATCHER and Mary Walthall, dau. of Gerrard Walthall who consents. This is consent only. Married 13 February by Rev. John Cameron, Rector Bristol Parish, Episcopal Church. p. 34.

2 July 1773. Jeremiah HATCHER and Edith Logwood. Consent of Edmund Logwood for Edith; no relationship stated. Sur. Josiah Hatcher. p. 2.

1 April 1808. Jesse HATCHER and Martha Laprade, dau. of A. Laprade, deceased. William Laprade, brother of Martha, consents for her. Sur. Henry Walthall, Jr. p. 90.

13 August 1783. Josiah HATCHER and Judith Flournoy, dau. of Jacob Flournoy who consents. Sur. Jacob Flournoy, Jr. Wit. Peter Clark. p. 19.

18 October 1809. Josiah W. HATCHER and Elizabeth Gary, dau. of David Gary who consents. Sur. Arthur Nunnally. p. 98.

7 December 1801. Obadiah HATCHER and Polley Beasley. Write their own consent. Wit. Robertson Beasley and William Beasley. This is consent only. Married by Rev. Eleazer Clay, Baptist. p. 64.

2 May 1789. Uriah HATCHER and Aggy Hatcher. Sur. Ezekiel Dance. Married 14 May by Rev. Needler Robinson, Rector of Dale Parish, Episcopal Church. p. 28.

11 January 1811. William HATCHER and Elizabeth Lafon, dau. of Thomas Lafon. Sur. Leonard Nunnally. p. 106.

25 May 1803. William HATCHETT and Tabitha Baugh, dau. of James Baush who consents. Sur. John Jackson. p. 67.

30 November 1804. Henry HAXALL and Jane Gray Shore. Sur. Joseph Haxall. p. 74.

10 September 1785. William HAXALL and Elizabeth Jones. Married by Rev. William Leigh, Rector of Manchester Parish, Episcopal Church. "License from Dinwiddie." Ministers' Returns p. 370.

12 March 1798. George HAZELTON and Amy Daniel, dau. of Thomas Daniel "late of England." Charles Purcell of Richmond, guardian of Amy consents for her. Sur. Jesse Hix. Wit. Lewis Buckner and Moses A. Lipscomb. p. 51.

4 January 1815. Henry HEATH and Eliza Ann Cunliffe, dau. of John Cunliffe who consents. Sur. Richard Booker. Wit. Charles Cunliffe. p. 128.

3 April 1805. Edward HENRY and Barbara Alvis, 21 years of age, dau. of Ann Alvis. Sur. Woodford Alvis. Wit. Edward Burnett. Married by Rev. Benjamin Watkins. p. 76.

14 December 1786. Dr. John HEVENINGHAM and Susanna Nivins. This is consent only. p. 25.

5 August 1786. William HICKMAN and Obedience Brown, dau. of George Brown who consents. This is consent only. Married 10 August by Rev. John Goode. p. 24.

15 February 1806. John W. HIGGINBOTHAM and Lucy Randolph, widow of Henry Randolph. Sur. T. M. Nelson. p. 81.

21 March 1805. Armstred (Armistead) HILL and Sally Cogbill. Married by Rev. Henry Featherstone, Sr. Ministers' Returns p. 397.

    March 1787. Benjamin HILL and Elizabeth Elam. Sur. David Elam, Jr. Married by Rev. Eleazer Clay, Baptist. p. 25.

66

3 September 1797. Benjamin HILL and Nancy Franklin. Sur.
Jacob Flournoy, Jr. Married 5 October by Rev. Benjamin Watkins.
p. 48.

13 May 1799. Edward HILL and Judith Chalkley, 23 years of age.
Sur. Olive Hill. Wit. Edward Hill. Married by Rev. Eleazer
Clay, Baptist. p. 55.

1 August 1795. James HILL and Dicey Blankenship. Sur. Archer
Winfree. Married by Rev. Eleazer Clay, Baptist. p. 41.

10 August 1798. James HILL and Nancy Worsham. Married by Rev.
Nathan Anderson, Methodist. Ministers' Returns p. 388.

9 December 1771. John HILL and Martha Cheatham. Sur. Jacob
Ashurst. p. 1.

3 September 1773. John HILL and Ann Dodson. Sur. Richard
Booker. p. 2.

15 July 1780. John HILL, Jr. and Anne Wilkinson. Sur. Richard
Wilkinson. p. 12.

16 May 1786. John HILL and Mary Worsham. Married by Rev.
William Leigh, Rector of Manchester Parish, Episcopal Church.
Ministers' Returns p. 370.

_____ 1787. John HILL and Ann Puckett. Married by Rev.
John Goode. Ministers' Returns p. 373.

3 December 1811. John HILL and Polly Winfree, dau. of Reuben
Winfree who consents. Sur. Francis Watkins. Married 5 December
by Rev. Benjamin Watkins. p. 111.

12 October 1778. William HILL and Sarah Cousins. Sur. George
Cousins. p. 7.

9 July 1784. William HILL and Jane Lockett. Sur. William
Lockett. p. 21.

22 July 1801. Anthony HINCKLE and Milly Roper, dau. of Drury
Roper who consents. Wit. Thomas Donnelly and Robert Anderson.
This is consent only. Married 25 July by Rev. Benjamin Watkins.
p. 63.

_____ 1790. John HIX and Anne Grant. Married by Rev.
Eleazer Clay, Baptist. Ministers' Returns p. 376.

18 January 1797. John HIX and Fanny Turner, dau. of Martha
Turner who consents. Sur. Matthew Turner. Wit. John Snellings.
Married by Rev. Eleazer Clay, Baptist. p. 46.

4 January 1805. John HIX and Polly Mitchell, 21 years of age.
Sur. Samuel Woody. Wit. Marice Brooks. Married 5 January by
Rev. Benjamin Watkins. p. 75.

3 December 1805. Josiah HIX and Levina Moore. Haley Cole,
uncle of "Vina" consents for her. Sur. Archibald Wooldridge.
Married by Rev. Eleazar Clay, Baptist. p. 79.

23 December 1805. William HIX and Betsy Morrissett, dau. of
Jane Morrissett who consents. Sur. Peter Morrissett. Wit.
William Elliott. Married by Rev. Eleazar Clay, Baptist. p. 80.

12 September 1803. Jeremiah HOBBS and Frances Godsey, dau. of
John Godsey, Senr. who consents. Sur. Henry Godsey. Wit.
Thomas Godsey. p. 68.

31 March 1810. Stephen HOBBS and Patsey Hatcher, 21 years of
age, dau. of Nathaniel Hatcher, deceased. Sur. William Hatcher.
Married 3 April by Rev. Thomas Lafon, Church of Christ. p. 101.

29 June 1788. James HODGE and Martha Ashbrook. Married by Rev.
Needler Robinson, Rector of Dale Parish, Episcopal Church.
Ministers' Returns p. 374.

8 September 1808. Samuel HART and Nancy Gibbon Walthall, dau.
of Archibald Walthall who consents and is surety. Married by
Rev. John Cox, Methodist. p. 92.

4 March 1810. John HODGES and Tabitha Flournoy, dau. of John
Flournoy, deceased. Josiah Flournoy, guardian of Tabitha
consents for her. Sur. William Laprade, Sr. p. 101.

10 February 1794. William T. HODGSON and Hannah Flournoy. Sur.
Henry Flournoy. Wit. William Cheatham. p. 38.

22 December 1806. Joseph HODSON and Mary Quarles, dau. of
Nathaniel Quarles who consents and is surety. p. 84.

12 January 1795. Valentine HOLDERFIELD and Esther Williams,
dau. of Frankey (Frances?) Williams who consents. Wit. James
Clark and John Clark. This is consent only. Married by Rev.
James Smith. p. 40.

1 December 1780. William HOLLIDGE and ____ ____. Sur. Ben Smith. p. 13.

14 October 1790. John HOOD and Elizabeth Osborne Downman, dau. of William Downman who consents. This is consent only. Married 30 October by Rev. John Cameron, Rector of Bristol Parish, Episcopal Church. p. 31.

13 July 1812. James B. HOOPER and Edith Hancock, dau. of George Hancock, deceased. Sur. William Hancock. Wit. Jeremiah Hancock. p. 115.

6 December 1785. John HOOPER and Mary Baker. This is consent only. Married by Rev. Eleazer Clay, Baptist. p. 23.

21 December 1809. John HOPKINS and Jane Clarke, dau. of Charles Clarke, Sr. who consents. Sur. Benjamin W. Layne. Wit. Maryan Sallee Clarke. p. 99.

20 December 1798. Lund HOPKINS and Mary H. Martin, dau. of William Martin who consents. Sur. Jordan Martin. Married 27 December by Rev. George Smith, Baptist. p. 53.

3 December 1784. William HOPKINS and Hamey Branch, dau. of Samuel Branch who consents. This is consent only. p. 22.

4 November 1789. Abijah HORNER and Patsie Sutberry, dau. of Ezekiel Sudberry who consents. This is consent only. Married 7 November by Rev. Needler Robinson, Rector of Dale Parish, Episcopal Church. p. 29.

16 December 1804. Arthur HORNER and Armenia Newby, dau. of Levi Newby who consents. Sur. Henry Walthall, Jr. p. 74.

____ ____ 1792. Benjamin HORNER and Mary Furguson. Married by Rev. Eleazer Clay, Baptist. Ministers' Returns p. 379.

11 July 1814. Benjamin HORNER and Rhoda Brummall, dau. of William Brummall who consents and is surety. Married 12 July by Henry Bridgewater. p. 125.

9 May 1808. Daniel HORNER and Mary Womack, dau. of Abram Womack, deceased. John Varnier, guardian of Mary, consents for her and is surety. p. 91.

29 October 1811. Ezekiel HORNER and Elizabeth Fuqua. John J. Kleinhoff, guardian of Elizabeth, consents for her. Sur. Major Horner. p. 110.

31 October 1812. Major HORNER and Kitturah Morgan. Lucy Morgan guardian of Kitturah, consents for her. Sur. John L. Morgan. Wit. Sarah Kleinhoff. p. 116.

29 December 1813. Samuel HORNER and Catharine Cross, dau. of Joseph Cross of King and Queen County. Sur. Reuben Cross. Married 30 December by Rev. Henry Bridgewater. p. 123.

21 April 1809. William HORNER and Polly Hamblin, 21 years of age, dau. of Charles Hamblin, deceased. Sur. William Beasley. p. 97.

1785-1786. Samuel HORTON and Mary Baugh. Married by Rev. Eleazer Clay, Baptist. Ministers' Returns p. 371.

28 February 1792. George HOUSE and Ann Wells. Married by Rev. John Cameron, Rector of Bristol Parish, Episcopal Church.

26 January 1811. John HOWARD and Lucy Cross, 21 years of age, dau. of Reuben Cross. Sur. Reuben Cross, Jr. p. 107.

10 January 1791. Rubin HOWARD and Nancy Hill. Sur. William Loafman. p. 32.

28 February 1815. Robert HOWELL and Mary Ann Edwards, dau. of Edward B. Edwards who consents. Sur. Samuel Bowman. p. 129.

9 January 1803. Thomas HOWLET and Martha Archer Branch. John Friend, guardian of Martha, consents for her. This is consent only. p. 66.

15 November 1808. Thomas HOWLETT and Elizabeth Boisseau, dau. of Daniel Boisseau who consents. p. 93.

___ June 1803. Anderson HOYE and Elizabeth Noble. Married by Rev. Henry Featherstone, Sr. Ministers' Returns p. 396.

20 December 1814. James O'Kelly HUBBARD and Lemiry Cheatham, dau. of Stephen Cheatham who consents. Sur. Erasmus Reams. Wit. Daniel Hudson. Married 24 December by Rev. Daniel Hudson. p. 127.

25 June 1784. Robert HUBBERD and Elizabeth Syree (Tyree?). Married by Rev. William Hickman, Minister of Skinquarter Baptist Church. Ministers' Returns p. 369.

HUDSON: See HUTSON

22 June 1812. Daniel HUDSON and Sally Stanford, widow of Thomas
Stanford. Sur. Parke Poindexter. She was Sally Wooldridge, dau.
of Edward Wooldridge. p. 114.

4 December 1778. Irby HUDSON and Phebe Featherstone. Sur.
Henry Featherstone. p. 7.

17 November 1812. Richard C. HUDSON and Page Farmer, dau. of
Hezekiah Farmer who consents. Sur. William C. Bass. p. 117.

19 November 1810. Benjamin HUGHES and Sarah Anderson, 21 years
of age. Sur. Thomas Anderson, Jr. Benjamin Hughes of Powhatan
County. p. 105.

8 November 1787. Richard HULETT and Mary Dunlavy. Wit. Daniel
Gordon. This is consent only. p. 26.

30 March 1780. Charles HUNDLEY and _____. Sur. Joseph
Jackson. p. 11.

1 February 1798. James HUNTER and Elizabeth Howlett. Sur.
John Howlett. James Hunter of Campbell County. p. 50.

17 September 1807. John HUTCHINGS and Tabitha Baker. This is
in an unsigned list in the Ministers' Returns. Ministers'
Returns p. 403.

20 February 1815. Conrad HUTSON and Nancy Chamberlain, 21
years of age. Sur. Lancelot Walker. Married 25 February by
Rev. Thomas Lafon who says Hudson. p. 128.

3 September 1781. Lewellin HUTSON and Rebecca Tatum, dau. of
Josiah Tatum. Sur. Francis Goode. Wit. Elizabeth Tatum. p. 14.

19 January 1790. Ralph HYLTON and Polly Ward. Robert Goode
consents for Polly; no relationship stated. This is consent
only. p. 30.

21 July 1792. Thomas IRWIN and Ann Franklyn. Married by Rev.
Richard Garrettson of Petersburg. Ministers' Returns p. 378.

20 November 1815. Bashford IRWIN and Sophia Gill, dau. of
Joseph Gill. Sur. Archibald Totty. Wit. Epps Gill. Married
22 November by Rev. Thomas Lafon, Church of Christ. p. 132.

13 March 1797. Abel JACKSON and Frances Gill. Married by Rev. Needler Robinson, Rector of Dale Parish, Episcopal Church. Ministers' Returns p. 385.

14 January 1797. Francis JACKSON and Rebekah Perry. Married by Rev. Thomas Hardie, Methodist. Ministers' Returns p. 385.

22 December 1789. Ezekiel JACKSON and Rhode Dance. Married by Rev. John Cameron, Rector of Bristol Parish, Episcopal Church.

_____ 1803. John JACKSON and Sarah Baugh. Married by Rev. Eleazar Clay, Baptist. Ministers' Returns p. 397.

8 December 1806. John R. JACKSON and Martha R. Jones, dau. of Eliza Jones who consents. Sur. John Vest. p. 83.

11 March 1793. Stewart JACKSON and Elizabeth Perry. Married by Rev. Needler Robinson, Rector of Dale Parish, Episcopal Church. Ministers' Returns p. 378.

15 January 1797. William JACKSON and Elizabeth Ball. Sur. Isham Ball. Wit. Thomas Finney. Married 26 January by Rev. James Rucks. p. 46.

24 March 1812. William JACKSON and Betsy Dance Jackson, dau. of Ezekiel Jackson who consents. Sur. Philip Cogbill. p. 113.

20 December 1804. William JAMES and Elizabeth Goode. Married by Rev. Charles Hopkins. Ministers' Returns p. 398.

7 September 1786. John JEFFRIES and Anne Elizabeth Jones. Married by Rev. John Cameron, Rector of Bristol Parish, Episcopal Church.

9 January 1804. Benjamin JENNINGS and Salley Boles, dau. of Henry Boles who consents. Wit. Arthur Boles and Parke Poindexter Married 12 Jan. by Rev. Benjamin Watkins. p. 70.

17 November 1800. Daniel JENNINGS and Martha Watkins, dau. of Mary Watkins who consents. Wit. Stephen Watkins. Daniel Jennings of Powhatan County. Married 20 November by Rev. Benjamin Watkins. p. 61.

23 May 1798. Edmund JENNINGS and Jemima Chappell, dau. of Ann Chappell who consents. Sur. Henry Godsey. Wit. Larkin Pilkinton and Daniel Jennings. Married 26 May by Rev. Benjamin Watkins. p. 52.

1 October 1806. Caleb JETER and Sally M. Cobb, dau. of Samuel Cobb, deceased. Sur. Abram S. Wooldridge. Married by Rev. Eleazar Clay, Baptist. p. 83.

4 April 1777. Samuel JETER and Mene Moody alias Ellyson. Sur. Thomas Branch. p. 5.

1801-1802. Anderson JOHNSON and Polley Cox. Married by Rev. Eleazar Clay, Baptist. Ministers' Returns p. 394.

14 December 1812. David JOHNSON and Elizabeth Lookado, 21 years of age. Sur. Edward Goode. p. 117.

24 December 1808. Hudson JOHNSON and Elizabeth Burton, dau. of William Burton who consents and is surety. Married by Rev. Benajmin Watkins. p. 94.

8 June 1790. Isaac JOHNSON and Edith Brummall. This is consent only. Married 26 June by Rev. Benjamin Watkins. p. 31.

15 September 1815. James JOHNSON and Hannah Cook, widow of William Cook. Sur. Edward Goode. Wit. James Blankenship. Married 16 September by Rev. Edmund Goode, Baptist. p. 131.

8 April 1805. John JOHNSON and Salley Gill, 21 years of age, dau. of Benjamin Gill who is surety. p. 76.

12 December 1814. John JOHNSON and Mary A. Wooldridge, dau. of Edward Wooldridge, deceased. Sur. Edward Wooldridge (brother). p. 127.

13 May 1794. Miles JOHNSON and Mary Totty. Married by Rev. Needler Robinson, Rector of Dale Parish, Episcopal Church. Ministers' Returns p. 378.

14 May 1801. Thomas W. JOHNSON and Amey Rudd. Married by Rev. Charles Forsee, Minister of Skinquarter Baptist Church. Ministers' Returns p. 395.

9 July 1810. Watson JOHNSON and Martha Burton, dau. of William Burton who consents. Sur. Edward Cary. Wit. John Burton. p. 103.

5 September 1803. William Thompson JOHNSON and Elizabeth Goode, dau. of William Goode who consents. Sur. John Johnson. Married 8 Sept. by Rev. Benjamin Watkins. p. 68.

24 February 1809. William JOHNSON and Nancy Hancock, 21 years of age, dau. of John Hancock. Sur. William Hancock. p. 96.

7 October 1813. William JOHNSON and Polly Burton, 21 years of age. Sur. John Burton. p. 122.

8 January 1813. David C. JONES and Sarah Kleinhoff. Sur. John Mann. Wit. John Morgan and Elizabeth R. Morgan. Married by Rev Henry Bridgewater. David C. Jones of Amelia County. Also given David B. Jones. p. 118.

4 September 1796. Francis JONES and Martha Field Walthall, dau of Archibald Walthall who consents. Wit. William Archer and John Friend. This is consent only. Married 6 October by Rev. Needler Robinson, Rector of Dale Parish, Episcopal Church. p. 45.

1 August 1783. John JONES and Elizabeth Danlavey. Wit. John Lawson. This is consent only. p. 18.

13 June 1786. Thomas Booker JONES and Rebeckah Edwards Jones. Wit. John Jones. This is consent only. This couple was married by Rev. John Cameron 15 June 1786. It is in his "Register of Marriages in Bristol Parish." He says Thomas Brooks Jones. p. 24.

19 April 1789. Thomas JONES and Elizabeth Baugh. Married by Rev. Needler Robinson, Rector of Dale Parish, Episcopal Church. Ministers' Returns p. 374.

10 February 1801. John JORDAN and Nelly Ro___ (mutilated). Married by Rev. George Smith, Baptist. Ministers' Returns p. 391.

3 March 1789. Lewis JUIT and Elizabeth Thomas. Sur. James Thomas. p. 27.

22 November 1815. Mordecai KEARNAL and Betsey Branch, dau. of Olive Branch (father) who consents, and is surety. p. 132.

___ _____ 1792. Curell KEEN and Elizabeth Davis. Married by Rev. Eleazer Clay, Baptist. Ministers' Returns p. 379.

17 May 1797. John KELLY and Lucy Chockley. Sur. David Chockley Wit. William Finney. Married 18 May by Rev. Thomas Hardie, Methodist. p. 47.

2 February 1811. Charles KENT and Sally Edmunds Walthall. Sur. Samuel Hart. Married 9 February by Rev. John Cox of Petersburg, Methodist. p. 107.

26 June 1794. John KERR and Polly Ellyson. Sur. Orange Owen. Married by Rev. James Smith. p. 39.

30 September 1803. John KERR and Susannah Stith Cogbill, 21 years old 16 May 1802. Lucy Cogbill gives affidavit as to the age of Susannah. Sur. John Dillon. Wit. Henry Dillon, Benjamin Smith and Joseph Dillon. See John Carr. p. 68.

22 December 1813. Mordeca KERRALD and Ona Walden. Sur. Daniel Broadie. Wit. William Shortt. Married 25 December by Rev. Thomas Lafon, Church of Christ. p. 123.

_____ 1791. James KETTON and Elizabeth Harris. Married by Rev. James Smith. Returned 10 March 1791. See James Kitton. Ministers' Returns p. 377.

25 October 1814. Jasper KIDD and Susanna Powell. Sur. Alexander Powell. p. 126.

20 January 1797. William KIMBROUGH and Polly Gordon, dau. of Barbara Leath of Manchester who consents. Wit. M. Gordon and Daniel Weisiger. This is consent only. See bond dated 27 January 1798. p. 46.

27 January 1798. William KINBROUGH and Polly Gordon. Sur. Daniel Weisiger. See consent dated 20 January 1797. p. 50.

5 July 1787. Robert KINCAID and Elizabeth Cary "of Ampthill." Dau. of Archibald and Mary (Randolph) Cary, both deceased. This is consent only. Elizabeth was born 1769. p. 26.

1 August 1796. Julius KING and Betsey Baugh, dau. of Burwell Baugh who consents. Wit. Edward De Sear. This is consent only. Married 25 August by Rev. Needler Robinson, Rector of Dale Parish, Episcopal Church. p. 44.

20 May 1790. John KIRKLAND and Agness Lee. Married by Rev. John Cameron, Rector of Bristol Parish, Episcopal Church.

8 February 1791. James KITTON and Betsy Harris, dau. of James and Ursula Harris who consent. Sur. Alexander Burnett. See James Ketton. p. 32.

27 August 1794. John Jocelyn KLEINHOFF and Sarah Morgan. Both of lawful age. Write their own consent. p. 39.

2 February 1809. John LABARREAIRE and Ann P. Cheatham, dau. of Isham Cheatham, deceased. Sur. William Gates. Wit. Charles Forsee. Married by Rev. Charles Forsee, Skinquarter Baptist Church. p. 95.

5 May 1795. John LABOREAR and Rebecca Roberts. Sur. William Roberts. Wit. William Finney. Married 9 May by Rev. Benjamin Watkins. p. 41.

30 December 1802. David LACEY and Nancy Farmer. Married by Rev. Charles Forsee, Minister of Skinquarter Baptist Church. Ministers' Returns p. 393.

3 December 1786. Archibald LACY and Sarah Martin. Married by Rev. John Goode. Ministers' Returns p. 371.

2 October 1810. Haulcoat LACY and Rhoda Moxley. Sur. Archibal Puckett. Married 3 October by Rev. Edmund Goode, Baptist. p. 104.

9 July 1812. Haucoat LACY and Elizabeth Beasley, dau. of Henry Beasley, deceased. Sur. Thomas Beasley. p. 114.

15 September 1812. Wilson LAIN and Matilda C. Morrissett, dau. of Daniel Morrissett, deceased. Daniel Wade, guardian of Matilda, consents for her. Sur. Richard K. Weiseger. p. 116.

_____ 1787. Lewis LAMBERT and Frances Moseley. Married by Rev. John Goode. Ministers' Returns p. 373.

9 March 1807. Thomas LAMBERT and Jinsey Smith. dau. of Benjami Smith who consents and is surety. p. 85.

27 January 1794. Levin LANDRUM and Mourning Hudson, dau. of Sarah Hudson who consents. Sur. John Hudson. Wit. Daniel Hudson. Married by Rev. James Smith of Powhatan County. p. 38

28 September 1810. James LANG and Mary Wood. Sur. Daniel Weisiger. Wit. J. Robertson. p. 104.

_____ 1792. William LANGFORD and Elizabeth Pankey. Married by Rev. Eleazer Clay, Baptist. Was she a widow? See marriage of Carter Moody and Sarah Pankey. Ministers' Returns p. 379.

LAPRADE: See LEPRADE

22 May 1801. William Parin LAW and Martha Dance. Married by Rev. Henry Featherstone, Sr. See W. Parrenglaw. Ministers' Returns p. 392.

1 April 1773. John LAWTEN and Nanney Blaikley. Sur. William Blaikley, Jr. See John Lorton. p. 2.

14 January 1787. Peter LEATH and Barbara Gordon. This is consent only. She must have been a widow. See George Penn, Jr.; also William Kimbrough. p. 25.

6 September 1805. Lewis LEE and Susannah Winfree. James Winfree, guardian of Susannah consents for her. Sur. Francis Winfree. Wit. Ann M. Winfree and Robert Blakey. Married 7 September by Rev. Charles Hopkins. p. 78.

24 November 1812. Jeptha LEET and Elizabeth Bass, 21 years of age, dau. of Edward Bass, Sr. Sur. Daniel Bass. Wit. John Porter. p. 117.

24 December 1802. Benjamin W. LEIGH and Mary Selden Watkins. Married by Rev. Needler Robinson, Rector of Dale Parish, Episcopal Church. Ministers' Returns p. 391.

21 December 1798. Andrew LEPRADE and Ann Kelcher. Sur. William Lankford. Wit. Thomas Finney. Married by Rev. Eleazer Clay, Baptist, who says Laprade. p. 53.

8 December 1785. John LEPRADE and Phebe Elam. Married by Rev. William Leigh, Rector of Manchester Parish, Episcopal Church. Ministers' Returns p. 370.

21 March 1797. John LEPRADE and Sally Snellings, dau. of Alexander Snellings who consents. Sur. Martin Brooks. Married by Rev. Eleazer Clay, Baptist. p. 47.

9 June 1781. Martell LESEUR and Elizabeth Bacon. Sur. Enos Ellyson. p. 14.

_____ 1792. Jacob LESTER and Annuse Cayce. Married by Rev. Eleazer Clay, Baptist. See Jacob Luster. Ministers' Returns p. 379.

17 January 1799. Robert LESTER and Elizabeth H. Moseley, dau. of Richard Moseley who consents. Sur. James Hill. Wit. Henry Moseley and Thomas Moseley. p. 54.

19 August 1806. Moses LEVI and Caroline Dunnavant, dau. of William Dunnavant who consents and is surety. p. 82.

12 November 1789. John LIGON and Jinsey Dunavant. Sur. Richard Baugh. Married 24 November by Rev. Needler Robinson, Rector of Dale Parish, Episcopal Church who says Jean. p. 29.

15 May 1786. Thomas LIVELY and Phebe Steward. Married by Rev. William Leigh, Rector of Manchester Parish. Episcopal Church. Ministers' Returns p. 370.

4 March 1802. Charles LOCKETT and Nancy Hix. Married by Rev. Benjamin Watkins. Ministers' Returns p. 396.

17 November 1783. David LOCKETT and Mary Ashbrook, dau. of Joseph Ashbrook who consents. Sur. Peter Ashbrook. p. 19.

11 May 1796. Elam LOCKETT and Phebe Cheatham, dau. of Elizabeth Cheatham who consents. Wit. Francis Cheatham. This is consent only. p. 44.

16 May 1783. Francis LOCKETT, Jr. and _____ Wooldridge, dau. of Thomas Wooldridge of "Swift Creek" who consents. This is consent only. p. 18.

10 December 1810. James LOCKETT and Gilley Mann, dau. of Branch Mann who consents. Sur. George Snellings. p. 105.

12 January 1807. Obadiah LOCKETT and Sarah Cox, 21 years of age Sur. John Cox. Wit. Nathaniel Cary. p. 85.

1797-1798. Walthall LOCKETT and Obedience Hancock. Married by Rev. Eleazer Clay, Baptist. Ministers' Returns p. 387.

17 December 1792. John J. LOCKIN and Priscilla Cacy, dau. of Charles Casy who consents. Wit. Samuel Cobbs. This is consent only. See John Lockley. p. 35.

_____ _____ 1792. John LOCKLEY and Priscilla Cayce. Married by Rev. Eleazer Clay, Baptist. See John Lockin. Ministers' Returns p. 379.

15 May 1776. Archibald LOGWOOD and Ann Friend. Sur. Jeremiah Hatcher. p. 5.

1 April 1773. John LORTON and Nanny Blaikley. Sur. William Blaikley, Jr. See John Lawten. p. 2.

___ March 1800. Richard LOVIN and Mary Gill, dau. of Joseph Gill who consents. Wit. John Smith and Benjamin Gill. This is consent only. p. 60.

3 December 1811. Drury L. LUCADOE and Mary A. Bridgewater. Sur. Samuel Bridgewater. Married 5 December by Rev. Benjamin Watkins. p. 111.

___ _____ 1787. Jacob LUSTER and Martha Miles. Married by Rev. John Goode. Ministers' Returns p. 372.

13 November 1792. Jacob LUSTER and Anusze Cacy. Wit. Guleelmus Wood and Catherine Cacy. This is consent only. See Jacob Lester. p. 35.

10 June 1796. James LYLE and Sally B. Goode, dau. of Robert Goode who consents. Wit. Theodorick Goode. This is consent only. p. 44.

27 May 1809. James LYNCH, Jr. and Jinsey Andrews, dau. of Isham and Mary Andrews who consent. Sur. Isham Belcher. Wit. Fanny Andrews. p. 97.

1 June 1779. James McALISTER and Margaret McCallican. Sur. Colin Ferguson. Wit. George Markham. p. 9.

17 March 1788. James McALPIN and Elizabeth Aldridge (widow). Wit. B. Huds. (Hudson?). This is consent only. Married 5 April by Rev. Needler Robinson, Rector of Dale Parish, Episcopal Church. p. 26.

21 July 1812. John McCOLLUM and Mary Hardiman. Sur. James Winfree. p. 115.

14 May 1788. William McCRAW and Winifred Hill, dau. of Winifred Tatum who consents. Wit. Josiah Tatum, James Hix. This is consent only. p. 26.

14 January 1799. William McCRAW and Ann Robertson. Sur. John Brander. p. 54.

9 April 1792. William McDOWELL and Susanna Baugh. Married by Rev. Needler Robinson, Rector of Dale Parish, Episcopal Church. Ministers' Returns p. 377.

6 October 1780. James McGRAW and Jane (illegible). This is consent only. p. 12.

6 January 1815. Wade S. McGRUDER and Polly Stanford, 21 years
of age, dau. of David Stanford. Sur. John Stanford. Wit.
Daniel Hudson. Married 7 January by Rev. Daniel Hudson. p.
128.

30 March 1790. Alexander McKEEVER and Sally Jones. Married by
Rev. John Cameron, Rector of Bristol Parish, Episcopal Church.

7 March 1780. William McKENZIE and Martha Harrison, dau. of
William Harrison, deceased. William Harrison, guardian of
Martha consents dated 18 March 1780. Sur. Robert Harris. Wit.
Andrew Harrison. She is called Patsey in consent. p. 11.

22 August 1807. James McKINNEY and Salley Scott, dau. of John
Scott who consents and is surety. p. 87.

21 March 1790. Alexander McKOWN and Sally Jones, dau. of John
Jones who consents. Wit. Nathaniel Jones. This is consent
only. p. 30.

25 July 1787. Daniel McLAURIN and Susannah Edwards. Married by
Rev. John Cameron, Rector of Bristol Parish, Episcopal Church.

21 May 1802. Jared McMASTERS and Mary Smith, dau. of James
Smith who consents. Sur. John Hancock and Joseph Moles. Wit.
Richard Taylor and Patrick Ogilby. Married by Rev. Henry
Featherstone, Sr. p. 65.

27 November 1791. John McMICAH and Phebe Perkenson. Married by
Rev. Needler Robinson, Rector of Dale Parish, Episcopal Church.
Ministers' Returns p. 377.

27 January 1796. Charles James McMURDO and Catherine Anna
Cochrane. Consent of J. Wardrop for Catherine "nearest relation
and guardian." Sur. Daniel Gay. Wit. William Burch. p. 43.

18 October 1808. Allen McRAE and Lucy B. Saunders, dau. of
Susanna Moseley who consents. Sur. Parke Poindexter. Wit.
Edward Moseley, Sr. and Archibald L. Wooldridge. p. 93.

27 June 1799. Archibald McRAE and Tabitha Randolph Cox.
Married by Rev. Needler Robinson, Rector of Dale Parish, Episcopal Church. Ministers' Returns p. 390.

26 April 1804. Collin McRAE and Ann Field Graves, dau. of
Charles Graves who consents. Sur. Thomas Graves. Married by
Rev. Needler Robinson, Rector of Dale Parish, Episcopal Church
who says Colin. p. 72.

22 October 1798. Robert McTYRE and Urcilla or Usly Martin (probably Ursula), widow of William Martin. Sur. James Winfree, Jr. Wit. T. Finney and Ursula Martin. Robert McTyre of Richmond. p. 53.

4 December 1778. Matthew McVEA and Elizabeth Keys. Sur. Thomas Bridgewater. p. 7.

29 May 1783. Charles MABRY and Phebe Gibbs. Sur. William Gibbs. p. 18.

25 January 1814. Henry MACHEN and Nancy Wilkinson, 21 years of age. Sur. Richard Wilkinson. Henry Machen of Prince George County. p. 123.

13 November 1792. Zepheniah MAGRUDA and Frances Sublett. Lewis Sublett consents for Frances. No relationship stated. This is consent only. p. 35.

1785-1786. Tapley MAHANES and Dinah Cheatham. Married by Rev. Eleazer Clay, Baptist. Ministers' Returns p. 371.

1 January 1803. John MAHONE and Jane Paul. See John R. Mehone. p. 485.

11 February 1805. John MAHONE and Nancy Miles. Sur. John Miles. Married 21 February by Rev. Benjamin Watkins. p. 75.

6 February 1784. Peter MAHONE and Mary Ann Flournoy. See Peter Mehone. p. 485.

12 April 1813. Jeremiah MALE and Milly Andrews, 21 years of age. Sur. Isham Belcher. Married 17 April by Rev. Joseph Gill, Jr. Spelled Mail in bond and Mael in Ministers' Returns. p. 120.

12 October 1801. Joseph MALE and Jensey Handcock. Wit. Polly Handcock. This is consent only. p. 63.

5 October 1809. Robert MALE and Jinsey Traylor, dau. of Daniel Traylor who consents. Sur. Joseph Traylor. Wit. Catherine Male. p. 98.

14 April 1802. John MANLY and Hororiah Conbusia. Wit. Herbert Claiborne. This is consent only. p. 65.

9 December 1798. Cain MANN and Mary Wilson, dau. of Edward and Caty Wilson who consent. This is consent only. Married 10 January 1799 by Rev. Thomas Hardie, Methodist. p. 53.

19 May 1810. Cain MANN and Nancy Anderson, 21 years of age, dau. of William Anderson, deceased. Sur. William Anderson. p. 102.

7 December 1811. Cain MANN and Elizabeth Newby. Sur. Levi Newby. p. 111.

25 March 1799. Ephraim MANN and Johana Berry. Married by Rev. Thomas Hardie, Methodist. Ministers' Returns p. 389.

4 December 1815. Francis MANN and Appy Snellings, dau. of James Snellings who consents. Sur. George H. Moore. Married 9 December by Rev. Joseph Gill, Jr. p. 132.

17 September 1796. John MANN and Mary Archer. Married by Rev. Thomas Hardie, Methodist. Ministers' Returns p. 383.

11 April 1798. John MANN and Fanny Rowlett. Married by Rev. Thomas Hardie, Methodist. Ministers' Returns p. 388.

18 October 1806. John MANN and Agnes Perkinson, dau. of Baxter Perkinson. Sur. David Perkinson. p. 83.

___ July 1800. Joseph MANN and Sally Anderson, dau. of Jerusha Anderson who consents. Wit. Elizabeth Mann and Rhoda Gill. This is consent only. Married by Rev. Eleazer Clay, Baptist. p. 60.

17 December 1807. Josiah MANN and Susannah Dunnavant. This is in an unsigned list in the Ministers' Returns. Ministers' Returns p. 403.

30 December 1785. Olive MANN and Prissy Berry. Married by Rev William Leigh, Rector of Manchester Parish, Episcopal Church. Ministers' Returns p. 370.

27 October 1785. Robert MANN and Molly Mann. Married by Rev. William Leigh, Rector of Manchester Parish, Episcopal Church. Ministers' Returns p. 369.

3 May 1813. Shastain MANN and Phebe Blankenship, dau. of Stephen Blankenship who consents. Sur. Beverly Stanley. Marrie 6 May by Rev. Joseph Gill, Jr. p. 120.

31 July 1813. Thomas H. MANN and Judith H. Bass, dau. of Edward Bass, deceased, and Judith Bass who consents. Sur. Parke Poindexter. Wit. John Mann, Jr. and Sally Cheatham. p. 121.

23 December 1801. Vincent MANN and Pheby Fargus. Married by Rev. Needler Robinson, Rector of Dale Parish, Episcopal Church, who says Phebe. Ministers' Returns p. 390.

3 June 1794. William MANN and Elizabeth Branch, dau. of Lucy Branch who consents. Sur. Edward Branch. p. 39.

21 August 1794. William MANN and Betty Gill. Sur. Robert Mann. p. 39.

21 February 1799. Worsham MANN and Anne Wilson. Married by Rev. Thomas Hardie, Methodist. Ministers' Returns p. 389.

25 February 1808. Edward MARABLE and Sally Moody, dau. of Samuel Moody who consents. Sur. Thomas Stratton. Married 27 February by Rev. Henry Featherstone, Sr. p. 89.

27 February 1808. Bernard MARKHAM and Elizabeth Osborne. Wit. Jeremiah Johnson and Samuel Mann. This is consent only. p. 89.

11 April 1774. George MARKHAM and Sarah Hill. Sur. John Hill. p. 3.

11 July 1789. George MARKHAM and Mary Osborne. Married by Rev. Needler Robinson, Rector of Dale Parish, Episcopal Church. Ministers' Returns p. 374.

14 December 1807. Joseph MARSH and Lucy Dyer Andrews, both 21 years of age. Dau. of Isham Andrews, deceased. Sur. Eldridge Smith. Married by Rev. John Cox, Methodist. p. 88.

14 July 1787. Alexander MARSHALL and Anne Walthall, dau. of Gerrard Walthall who consents. This is consent only. Married by Rev. John Cameron, Rector of Bristol Parish, Episcopal Church. p. 26.

6 June 1806. John MARSHALL and Sarah Branch, dau. of Edward Branch who consents. Sur. Edward O. Branch. p. 82.

24 January 1810. Samuel MARSHALL and Elizabeth G. Marshall, dau. of Alexander Marshall, Sr., deceased. John Stratton, guardian of Elizabeth, consents for her. Sur. Alexander Marshall. p. 100.

1 April 1774. William MARSHALL and Hannah Cobb. Sur. Thomas Worsham. p. 3.

June 1786-June 1787. James MARTIN and Jane Bryant. Married by Rev. Eleazer Clay, Baptist. Ministers' Returns p. 372.

31 March 1807. James MARTIN and Elizabeth Baker, dau. of John Baker. Sur. Samuel Bridgewater. Wit. John Hutchings. p. 86.

6 August 1801. John MARTIN and Milley Russell, dau. of Frances Russell who consents. Wit. Peterfield Russell and Stephen Russell. This is consent only. Married 8 August by Rev. Benjamin Watkins. p. 63.

6 December 1804. John MARTIN and Lucy Burke, widow of William Burke. Sur. Richardson Harris. Married 8 December by Rev. Benjamin Watkins. p. 74.

7 June 1810. John MARTIN and Lucy Wilkinson, dau. of John Wilkinson who consents. Sur. John Perdue. Wit. Richard Wilkinson. Married 9 June by Rev. Thomas Lafon, Church of Christ. p. 102.

5 June 1809. Jordan MARTIN and Martha Bass, 21 years of age, dau. of Judith Bass who consents. Sur. Thomas H. Bass. Married 8 June by Rev. Benjamin Watkins. p. 97.

21 July 1801. Royall MARTIN and Ann F. Logwood. Sur. John Friend. Wit. John Cary. Married 23 July by Rev. George Smith, Baptist. p. 63.

8 September 1778. Thomas MARTIN and Amey Bowman. Sur. John Bowman. p. 7.

6 September 1779. William MARTIN and Margaret Broodie. Daniel Weisiger, guardian of Margaret, consents for her. Sur. George Markham. p. 10.

21 April 1812. William MARTIN and Charlotte Robiou, dau. of Thomas F. Robiou who consents. His letter is dated 19 March 1812 Willis's River, Cumberland County. Sur. Samuel Bridgewater p. 113.

2 July 1812. William MARTIN and Martha Bailey, dau. of James and Elizabeth Bailey who consent. Sur. Elisha Bailey. p. 114.

3 November 1801. John MAXEY, Jr. and Lucy Anderson, dau. of Edward Anderson who consents. Wit. Nathaniel Anderson. This is consent only. p. 64.

2 April 1808. Edward A. May and Polly Hodges, dau. of James Hodges, deceased. John Friend, guardian of Polly, consents for her and is surety. Wit. George Cox. Married 8 April by Rev. Henry Featherstone, Sr. p. 90.

25 January 1814. Edward A. MAY and Sally Phillips Burton, dau. of Richard Burton who consents. Sur. Jesse W. Burton. Wit. Edmund Burton. Married 27 January by Rev. Joseph Gill. Jr. p. 123.

28 January 1815. Elijah MAY and Sarah Antonnette Nece. Sur. Parke Poindexter. p. 132.

_____ 1803. James MEGEE and Ann Hatcher. Married by Rev. Eleazar Clay, Baptist. Ministers' Returns p. 397.

1 February 1803. John R. MEHONE and Jane Paul, dau. of Elizabeth Skelton who consents. Sur. Claiborne Norris. Wit. William Morgan. p. 67.

6 February 1784. Peter MEHONE and Maryann Flournoy. Consent of Gipson Flournoy for Maryann; no relationship stated. Sur. John Laprade. See Peter Mohone. p. 20.

1796-1797. Philip MICALS and Mary B. Cobbs. Married by Rev. Eleazer Clay, Baptist. Ministers' Returns p. 386.

27 October 1808. John MICHAEL and Mason Male, dau. of Frederick Male who consents, and is surety. Married by Rev. John Cox, Methodist. p. 93.

8 August 1796. Phillips MICHALS and Mary B. Cobbs, dau. of Samuel Cobbs who consents. Wit. John Cobbs. This is consent only. p. 44.

20 September 1797. James MILES and Margaret Clibourne, of lawful age. Leonard Cliborne, brother of Margaret, consents for her. Sur. Enock Roberts. Wit. William Goodwin. Married by Rev. James Rucks. Returned 21 October. p. 48.

9 August 1800. John MILES and Hannah Leprade. Married by Rev. Benjamin Watkins. Ministers' Returns p. 390.

6 September 1800. David M. MILLER and Mary Watkins. This is consent only. Married 27 September by Rev. Henry Featherstone, Sr. p. 61.

8 December 1809. Hugh Melville MILLER and Mary Goode, 21 years of age, dau. of William Goode. Sur. Obadiah Winfree. Wit. John F. Morrisett. p. 99.

6 August 1784. Thomas MILLER and Ann Ball. Sur. Matthew Cheatham. p. 21.

25 August 1807. William MILLER and Ann Bottom, dau. of Mary Bottom who consents. Sur. Reuben Bottom. p. 87.

16 November 1786. Henry MILLS and Sarah Womack. Married by Rev. John Goode who says Hennery. Ministers' Returns p. 371.

8 August 1805. Nicholas MILLS and Sarah Ronald, dau. of Andrew Ronald, deceased. William Fenwick, guardian of Sarah consents and is surety. p. 77.

20 September 1797. Randolph MIMS and Elizabeth Cobbs, dau. of Samuel Cobbs who consents. This is consent only. Married 23 September by Rev. Benjamin Watkins. p. 48.

6 February 1784. Peter MOHONE and Maryann Flournoy. Consent of Gipson Flournoy for Maryann; no relationship stated. Sur. John Laprade. See Peter Mehone. p. 20.

18 July 1776. Jeremiah MOLES and Lydda Smith, dau. of Richard and Hannah Smith. Sur. Stephen Pankey. Wit. Stephen Pankey, J p. 5.

11 August 1813. Carter MOODY and Sarah Pankey, 21 years of age dau. of Elizabeth Lankford. Sur. John L. Morgan. p. 121.

1 January 1779. Enos MOODY and Mildred Bacon. Sur. Onan Moody p. 8.

3 August 1774. James MOODY and Amey Branch. Sur. George Markham. p. 4.

28 June 1792. James MOODY and Nancy Gibbons. Married by Rev. Stephen Davis. Ministers' Returns p. 378.

8 November 1813. James MOODY, Jr. and Mary Taylor. Sur. Parke Poindexter. Married 18 November by Rev. Thomas Anderson. p. 122.

16 December 1793. Sterling MOODY and Mary Nunnally. Sur. Jose Gates. Married 21 December by Rev. James Rucks. p. 37.

8 February 1808. William H. MOODY and Mary Atkins, dau. of Thomas Atkins who consents. Sur. John Moody. Married by Rev. Henry Featherstone, Sr. p. 89.

13 December 1808. Alexander MOORE and Phebe Mann, widow of Vincent Mann. Sur. Martin Davis. p. 94.

31 December 1790. Benjamin MOORE and Anne Kempton. Sur. Henry Beazley. p. 31.

1 August 1783. David MOORE and ____ ____. Sur. Henry Archer.
David son of John Moore. p. 18.

____ ____ 1790. Drewry MOORE and Lucy Gates. Married by Rev.
John Goode. Return dated 6 April 1790. Ministers' Returns p.
376.

23 December 1813. Edward MOORE and Lucy H. Dance, dau. of
Ezekiel Dance who consents and is surety. Married by Rev. Thomas
Lafon, Church of Christ. p. 123.

29 October 1796. Frederick MOORE and Sarah Nunnally. Sur.
Thornton Moore. Married 8 November by Rev. Thomas Hardie,
Methodist. p. 45.

5 September 1804. Frederick MOORE and Jane Dunnivant, 21 years
of age. Sur. Daniel Dunnivant. p. 73.

8 February 1796. George MOORE and Nancy Andrews, dau. of
Silvester Andrews who consents. This is consent only. Married
20 February by Rev. Needler Robinson, Rector of Dale Parish,
Episcopal Church. p. 43.

____ ____ 1789. Haskins (?) MOORE and Prudence Nunnally.
Married by Rev. John Goode. Ministers' Returns p. 375.

26 December 1799. James MOORE and Nancy Clarke. Married by
Rev. Benjamin Watkins. Ministers' Returns p. 390.

19 February 1812. James MOORE and Patsey Lookadoo, 21 years of
age. Sur. James Alvis. Wit. Archibald Shortt and John Moore.
p. 112.

23 April 1812. James MOORE and Sally Traylor. Sur. William
Traylor. Married 30 April by Rev. Joseph Gill, Jr. p. 114.

20 August 1804. John MOORE and Elizabeth Hancock, dau. of
Annanias Hancock. Sur. James Moore. Married 24 August by Rev.
Benjamin Watkins. p. 77.

26 July 1799. Pleasant MOORE and Nancy Goode, dau. of William
Goode who consents. Sur. Edward Cary. Wit. William Finney.
p. 56.

8 January 1784. Ralph MOORE and Faney Russell. Married by Rev.
William Hickman, Minister of Skinquarter Baptist Church.
Ministers' Returns p. 369.

____ ____ 1787. Richard MOORE and Edie Rucks. Married by
Rev. John Goode. Ministers' Returns p. 372.

20 November 1783. William MOORE and Jiney Vest. Married by Re
William Hickman, Ministers of Skinquarter Baptist Church.
Ministers' Returns p. 369.

28 November 1806. John Lewis MORGAN and Mary Fuqua, dau. of Jo
Fuqua, deceased. John J. Kleinhoff, guardian of Mary, consents
for her. Sur. James Martin, Jr. Wit. Ambrose Alexander. p. 8

22 March 1810. Thomas MORRIS and Basha Moore, 21 years of age,
dau. of Asa Moore. Sur. Thomas Cheatham. Married 27 March by
Rev. Charles Forsee, Skinquarter Baptist Church. p. 101.

25 March 1812. David MORRISETT and Polly Kelton, dau. of James
Kelton who consents. Sur. William Sublett. William Ellett,
guardian of David, consents for him. p. 113.

_____ 1803. Peter MORRISET and Elizabeth Elliot. Marrie
by Rev. Eleazar Clay, Baptist. Ministers' Returns p. 397.

2 April 1773. Alexander MOSELEY and Mary Cheatham. Sur.
Matthew Parkinson. Wit. Benjamin Watkins. p. 2.

3 November 1783. Benjamin MOSELEY and Mary Branch. Sur. Peter
Branch. p. 19.

26 January 1787. Edward MOSELEY and Rebecah Lewis, dau. of
Joseph Lewis who consents. This is consent only. Edward
Moseley of Powhatan County. p. 29.

20 December 1783. John MOSELEY and Elizabeth Rose. Consent of
Burwell Baugh (for both?). Sur. George Markham. p. 20.

15 October 1792. Peter MOSELEY and Polly Branch. Sur. John
Branch. p. 34.

1794-1795. Peter MOSELEY and Nancy West. Married by Rev.
Eleazer Clay, Baptist. Ministers' Returns p. 382.

8 October 1799. William MOSELEY and Salley Turpin, dau. of Ann
Turpin who consents. Sur. James Gayle. Wit. A. Haskins and
John Cary. Married 11 October by Rev. Benjamin Watkins. p. 56

7 January 1792. John MOSLEY and Nancy Folks. Married by Rev.
John Cameron, Rector of Bristol Parish, Episcopal Church.

18 October 1803. James MOXLEY and Mimey Puckett. Sur. Rolling Puckett. p. 69.

24 November 1807. Richard MOXLEY and Mariah Dodson. John Paul consents for Mariah; no relationship stated. Sur. William Morgan. Ministers' Returns say Mary. p. 88.

5 May 1780. John MURCHIE and Catey Harrison. Sur. William McKenzie. Wit. Robert Harris. Probably dau. of William Harrison, deceased, and sister of Martha who married William McKenzie. p. 11.

17 December 1812. Michael K. MURRY and Eliza Cabell. Sur. Edward Archer. p. 118.

24 November 1812. Claiborne NASH and Polly Adams, 21 years of age. Sur. William Smith. p. 117.

8 November 1803. Moses NASH and Nancy Barber. Married by Rev. Henry Featherstone, Sr. Ministers' Returns p. 396.

13 April 1810. William NASH and Margaret Anderson, 21 years of age, dau. of Janett Anderson. Sur. William Pool. Wit. Edward Burnett and James Burnett. p. 101.

22 October 1812. Samuel NELSON and Polly Adams, 21 years of age. Sur. John VICKERS. Married 23 October by Rev. Henry Bridgewater. p. 116.

6 April 1808. Edmund NEWBY and Teina Newby, dau. of Levi and Sarah (Farguson) Newby, who consent. Sur. Daniel Farguson. Both 21 years of age. Married 7 April by Rev. (this list is unsigned.). P. 90.

30 Karch 1782. Elijah NEWBY and Judith Farmer. Sur. George Markahm. p. 16.

13 March 1809. Jeremiah NEWBY and Nancy Chappell, 21 years of age, dau. of Robert Chappell, deceased. Sur. James Howard. Married 18 March by Rev. Benjamin Watkins. p. 96.

_____ 1796. Jesse NEWBY and Rhoda Furguson. Married by Rev. Eleazer Clay, Baptist. Ministers' Returns p. 384.

17 December 1781. John NEWBY and Martha Fourqurean, dau. of John Fourqurean. (This name misspelled. Furcron in bond). p. 15.

_____ 1792. John NEWBY and Amith Newby. Married by Rev. Eleazer Clay, Baptist. Ministers' Returns p. 380.

20 November 1779. Levy NEWBY and Sarah Farguson. King Graves, guardian of Sarah, consents for her. Sur. James Baugh. Wit. George Markham. p. 10.

19 September 1810. Martin NEWBY and Ann P. Bowman, dau. of Pleasant Bowman. Sur. Granville Bowman. Married 2 September by Rev. Thomas Lafon, Church of Christ. p. 104.

12 May 1800. Nathaniel NEWBY and Polly Ann Forqurean, of lawful age, dau. of Judith Forquron who consents. This is consent only. Married by Rev. Eleazer Clay, Baptist. p. 60.

8 August 1803. Nathaniel NEWBY and Frances Newby. Sur. George Baugh. Married by Rev. Eleazar Clay, Baptist. p. 68.

_____ 1796. William NEWBY and Martha Adkins. Married by Rev. Eleazer Clay, Baptist. Ministers' Returns p. 384.

24 May 1805. John NOBLE and Mary Walthall, dau. of Elizabeth Walthall. Sur. Lodowick Hoy. p. 76.

27 May 1808. William NOBLE and Milley Perkinson, both 21 years of age. Dau. of William Perkinson, deceased. Sur. John H. Archer. Wit. Francis R. Gibbs. Married 3 June by Rev. John Cox Methodist. Double wedding! See Arbin Taylor. p. 91.

1 October 1772. Mark NOBLES and Susanna Hoy. Sur. John Pride. Wit. John Dance. p. 1.

11 July 1793. Lemuel NODEN and Winny Blankenship. Married by Rev. John Cameron, Rector of Bristol Parish, Episcopal Church.

27 January 1789. John NOELL and Angelica Cheatham, dau. of Richard Cheatham who consents. Sur. Poindexter Noell. Married by Rev. Eleazer Clay, Baptist. p. 27.

June 1788-June 1789. Poindexter NOELL and Margaret Chatham. Married by Rev. Eleazer Clay, Baptist. Ministers' Returns p. 373.

28 October 1796. Robert NOELL and Tabitha Cheatham, dau. of Robert Cheatham who consents. Wit. Poindexter Noell. Married by Eleazer Clay, Baptist. p. 45.

1801-1802. Claiborn NORRIS and Rebecca Cheatham. Married by Rev. Eleazar Clay, Baptist. Ministers' Returns p. 394.

11 May 1803. Joseph NORRISS and Michel Matilda Fargusson, dau. of Martha Fargusson who consents. Sur. Robert Fargusson. Married by Rev. Eleazar Clay, Baptist. p. 67.

21 December 1811. Arthur NUNNALLY and Betsey Hobbs, 21 years of age. Sur. Randolph Martin. p. 111.

___ May 1803. Charles NUNNALLY and Drusilla Brintle. Married by Rev. Henry Featherstone, Sr. Ministers' Returns p. 396.

8 June 1808. Claiborne Puckett NUNNALLY and Nancy Vest, dau. of Philip Vest, Sr. who consents. Sur. William Fergusson. Wit. Nancy Fergusson. p. 91.

6 September 1810. David NUNNALLY and Mickey Perkinson, 21 years of age, dau. of William Perkinson, deceased. Sur. Matthew Burfoot. Wit. David Evans, Young Patterson and Nancy Belcher. p. 104.

22 July 1794. Edward NUNNALLY and Fanny Bailey. Sur. James Bailey. Married 24 July by Rev. James Rucks. p. 39.

10 February 1785. Henry NUNNALLY and Elizabeth Clay. Sur. Uriah Hatcher. p. 22.

18 March 1815. James NUNNALLY and Catharine Horner. Jamima Horner, guardian of Catharine, consents for her. Sur. Major Horner. Married 19 March by Rev. Henry Bridgewater. p. 129.

12 August 1789. John NUNNALLY and Mary Trent. Married by Rev. Benjamin Watkins. Ministers' Returns p. 375.

14 January 1793. John NUNNALLY and Sally Wilson. Married by Rev. Needler Robinson, Rector of Dale Parish, Episcopal Church. Ministers' Returns p. 377.

25 August 1815. John NUNNALLY and Betsey Johnson, 21 years of age. Sur. James Hall. Married 26 August by Rev. Thomas Lafon, Church of Christ. p. 131.

23 October 1800. Josiah NUNNALLY and Salley Atkinson. Married by Rev. Benjamin Watkins. Ministers' Returns p. 393.

14 March 1799. Leonard NUNNALLY and Frances Beasley. Married by Rev. Thomas Hardie, Methodist. Ministers' Returns p. 389.

_____ _____ 1789. Robert NUNNALLY and Jemima Rudd. Married by Rev. John Goode. Ministers' Returns p. 375.

11 September 1815. William Branch NUNNALLY and Tabitha Horner.
Sur. John L. Morgan. Married 12 September by Rev. Henry Bridgewater. p. 131.

_____ 1792. John NURNERY and Patty Gill. Married by Rev.
Eleazer Clay, Baptist. Could this name be Nunnally? Ministers'
Returns p. 380.

8 March 1811. Josiah OLDS and Sarah Anderson, widow of Robert
Anderson. Sur. John Vicars. p. 107.

6 June 1810. Francis S. O'REILLEY and Ann Friend. Sur. Samuel
Patterson. p. 102.

13 February 1783. Benjamin OSBORNE and Mary Walthall. William
Downman, guardian of Mary, consents for her. p. 17.

23 July 1789. Francis OSBORNE and Martha Field Walthall.
Married by Rev. Needler Robinson, Rector of Dale Parish, Episcopal Church. Ministers' Returns p. 374.

17 June 1784. Philip OTT and Mary Wray. Sur. John Foulkes.
See Philip Watt. p. 21.

11 July 1805. Alexander S. OUTLAW and Jane T. Woodson. No
surety or witness given. p. 77.

14 May 1789. John OVERBY (?) and Ann Traylor. Married by Rev.
Needler Robinson, Rector of Dale Parish, Episcopal Church.
Ministers' Returns p. 374.

2 April 1794. Orange OWEN and Nancy Ellyson. Sarah Bacon, aunt
of Nancy, consents for her. Sur. Edward Branch. Married by Rev
James Smith of Powhatan County. p. 38.

June 1787-June 1788. William Owen and Nancy Laprade. Married
by Rev. Eleazer Clay, Baptist. Ministers' Returns p. 372.

4 April 1783. Carter PAGE and Mary Cary, dau. of Archiblad Cary
who consents. Sur. Thomas Mann Randolph. Archibald Cary 1721-
1785 m. Mary Randolph 1727-1781. p. 18.

7 March 1787. Elijah PALMORE and Mary Ann Pride Cheatham.
Married by Rev. John Goode. In a list returned 1788. See John
Palmour. Members' Returns p. 373.

7 March 1787. Elijah PALMOUR and Elizabeth P. Cheatham. Sur.
Jesse Puckett. See Elijah Palmore. p. 25.

8 October 1798. Samuel PANKEY and Mary (Polly) Burton, dau. of Sarah Burton who consents. Wit. Charles Burton and Benjamin Jennings. This is consent only. Married 11 Oct. by Rev. Benjamin Watkins. p. 52.

18 October 1781. William PARHAM and Mary Branch. Sur. Edward Branch. p. 15.

22 May 1801. W. PARRENGLAW and Martha Dance, dau. of Edward Dance who consents. This is consent only. See William Parin Law. p. 62.

27 December 1792. John PARTER and Polly Elam. Married by Rev. James Rucks. See John Porter. Ministers' Returns p. 178.

2 April 1789. James PARTIN and Amy Totty. Married by Rev. Needler Robinson, Rector of Dale Parish, Episcopal Church. Ministers' Returns p. 374.

14 March 1808. Robert PARTIN and Lockey Rowlett, widow of John Rowlett. Sur. Herbert Brown. p. 90.

11 October 1785. James PARTING and Martha Tucker. William Parting, father of James, consents for him. Married 21 Oct. by Rev. William Leigh, Rector of Manchester Parish, Episcopal Church who says Partin. p. 23.

27 November 1815. Benjamin PATRAM and Sarah Taylor, 21 years of age. Sur. John Rowlett. Married 29 November by Rev. Joseph Gill, Jr. who says Benjamin A. Patram. p. 132.

17 March 1815. George PATRAM and Barbara Cole, both 21 years of age. Sur. Joshua White. Married 18 March by Rev. Joseph Gill, Jr. p. 129.

4 February 1796. John PATRAM and Elizabeth Perdue. Sur. William Puckett. Wit. William Finney and Thomas Finney. Married by Rev. Eleazer Clay, Baptist. p. 43.

9 October 1805. Peter PATRAM and Mary Worsham, 21 years of age, dau. of William Worsham, deceased. Sur. Francis Patram. p. 78.

22 August 1800. John PAUL and Polly Morgan. Married by Rev. Thomas Hardie, Methodist. Ministers' Returns p. 391.

1 January 1812. William PAUL and Sally Smith, dau. of William Smith who consents and is surety. p. 112.

19 October 1810. John PEARCE and Sarah Wilkinson, 21 years of age. Sur. William Goff. Wit. Morgan Pearce. p. 105.

30 June 1784. John PECK and Nancy Adams. Wit. Daniel Gordon. This is consent only. John Peck is of Manchester, a peruke make p. 21.

23 November 1795. George PENN, Jr. and Sally Gordon, dau. of Barbara Leith who consents. Sur. William Brown. George Penn, Jr. of Patrick County. p. 42.

2 May 1795. Nathan PENNIX and Tabitha Rudd. Married by Rev. James Rucks. Ministers' Returns p. 383.

_____ _____ 1800. John PERDUE and Phebe Moore. Married by Rev Eleazar Clay, Baptist. Ministers' Returns p. 393.

10 September 1804. Peter PERDUE and Sarah Graves, widow of John Graves. Sur. James Moody. p. 73.

12 July 1809. Shadrach PERDUE and Polly Hatchett, 21 years of age, dau. of John Hatchett, deceased. Sur. William Hatchett. p. 98.

9 April 1804. Stephen PERDUE and Nancy Gill, dau. of Benjamin Gill who consents and is surety. p. 71.

1801-1802. Thomas PERDUE and Dicey Mann. Married by Rev. Eleazar Clay, Baptist. Ministers' Returns p. 394.

18 May 1810. Thomas PERDUE and Lavinia Wiatt (Wyatt), 21 years of age. Sur. George Snellings. Married by Rev. Thomas Lafon, Church of Christ. p. 102.

29 December 1813. Anderson PERKINSON and Polly Perkinson, dau. of Willson Perkinson who consents and is surety. p. 123.

13 December 1787. Daniel PERKINSON and Mary Mann. Married by Rev. John Cameron, Rector of Bristol Parish, Episcopal Church.

18 December 1780. David PERKINSON and Mary Cobb. Sur. John Peery. See David Purkinson. p. 13.

8 April 1805. David PERKINSON and Betsy Perkinson, dau. of Ezekiel Perkinson who consents and is surety. Married by Rev. Eleazar Clay, Baptist. p. 76.

14 November 1792. Field PERKINSON and Priscilla Perkinson, dau.
of John Perkinson who consents for her and as uncle of Field
consents for him. This is consent only. Married 17 November by
Rev. John Cameron, Rector of Bristol Parish, Episcopal Church.
p. 35.

6 April 1793. Francis PERKINSON and Frances Andrews. Sur.
William Moore. Married 13 April by Rev. John Cameron, Rector of
Bristol Parish, Episcopal Church. p. 36.

3 November 1789. James PERKINSON and Beddy Andrews. Married by
Rev. Needler Robinson, Rector of Dale Parish, Episcopal Church.
Ministers' Returns p. 374.

24 December 1791. John PERKINSON and Elizabeth Anderson.
Married by Rev. John Cameron, Rector of Bristol Parish,
Episcopal Church.

7 March 1792. John PERKINSON and Lyncia Andrews. Sur. Berry
Andrews. Wit. James Perkinson. Married 10 March by Rev. John
Cameron, Rector of Bristol Parish, Episcopal Church. p. 34.

8 January 1805. John PERKINSON and Polley Dance, 21 years of
age, dau. of Baxwell Dance of Nottoway County. Sur. Worsham
Perkinson. p. 75.

3 January 1795. Joseph PERKINSON and Mary Davis Perkinson, dau.
of Robert Perkinson who consents. Joseph 21 years of age. This
is consent only. Married 8 January by Rev. Thomas Hardie,
Methodist. p. 40.

10 December 1804. Munford PERKINSON and Nancy Blankenship, dau.
of Drury Blankenship who consents and is surety. Married 18
December by Rev. Charles Forsee, Minister of Skinquarter Baptist
Church. p. 74.

25 July 1812. Peter Thomson PERKINSON and Dolly Gates, dau. of
William Gates who consents and is surety. Married by Rev.
Joseph Gill. Jr. p. 115.

27 March 1796. Robert PERKINSON and Patsey Perkinson. Married
by Rev. Thomas Hardie, Methodist. Ministers' Returns p. 383.

28 November 1808. Robert PERKINSON and Martha Perkinson, 21 years
of age, dau. of John Perkinson. Sur. Worsham Perkinson. p. 93.

14 March 1808. Thomas PERKINSON and Salley Willson, dau. of
Lodowick Willson. Sur. Thomas Willson. p. 90.

11 September 1804. Worsham PERKINSON and Edy Eanes, 21 years of
age. Sur. Richard Smith. Married by Rev. Henry Featherstone,
Sr. p. 73.

12 September 1789. James PERRY and Elizabeth Watkins. Married
by Rev. Needler Robinson, Rector of Dale Parish, Episcopal
Church. Ministers' Returns p. 374.

29 September 1798. Samuel PERRY and Elizabeth Jones. Married
by Rev. Thomas Hardie, Methodist. Ministers' Returns p. 386.

6 December 1788. William PERRY and Pheby Walthall. Married by
Rev. John Cameron, Rector of Bristol Parish, Episcopal Church.

17 September 1800. John PHAUP and ____ ____. p. 61.

29 October 1812. Anderson PHILIPS and Mary Andrews. Sur.
Isham Evans. Wit. Nancy Belcher. Married by Rev. Joseph Gill,
Jr. p. 116.

22 November 1810. Randolph PHILIPS and Rhoda Kelly, dau. of
Patrick Kelly who consents. Sur. John Harrold. Wit. Jesse
White. Married by Rev. Jordan Martin. p. 105.

June 1788-June 1789. Anderson PHILLIPS and Susanna Gill.
Married by Rev. Eleazer Clay, Baptist. Ministers' Returns p.
373.

24 December 1806. Reuben PICKETT and Betsy Hancock, 21 years of
age, dau. of John Hancock. Sur. William Hancock. p. 84.

21 April 1784. Larkin PILKINGTON and Sarah Chappell. Married
by Rev. William Hickman, Minister of Skinquarter Baptist Church.
Ministers' Returns p. 369.

_____ 1787. William PILKINGTON and Elizabeth Gates.
Married by Rev. John Goode. Ministers' Returns p. 372.

24 December 1797. William PILKINGTON and Polly Beasley.
Married by Rev. Nathan Anderson, Methodist. Ministers' Returns
p. 385.

2 April 1795. John PINCHBACK and Polly Rudd, dau. of Anne Rudd
who consents. Sur. Francis Foesee. Married 6 April by Rev.
James Rucks. p. 41.

17 July 1785. Thomas PINK and Betsy Loosey. Married by Rev. William Leigh, Rector of Manchester Parish, Episcopal Church. Ministers' Returns p. 369.

7 March 1787. Williamson H. PITMAN and Judith Watkins. Wit. Benjamin Watkins and Stephen Trabue. This is consent only. Married by Rev. Eleazer Clay, Baptist. p. 25.

20 February 1798. Williamson PITMAN and Eliza Goode. Married by Rev. James Rucks. Ministers' Returns p. 384.

8 May 1790. James PLEASANTS, Jr. and Susanna Rose, age 19. Sur. Philip Turpin. Wit. Charles Fleming and Martin Railey. p. 30.

21 September 1812. John PLEASANTS and Elizabeth Forsee, dau. of Charles Forsee who consents. Sur. John Forsee. Wit. Mary Forsee. p. 116.

1 November 1785. William PLEASANTS and Mary Frances Flournoy. Consent of Gipson Flournoy for Mary Frances; no relationship stated. This is consent only. Married 25 Nov. by Rev. William Leigh, Rector Manchester Parish, Episcopal Church. He says William Pleasant and Frances Flournoy. p. 23.

27 April 1808. Silvester PLUMB and Fanny Downman, dau. of Violet Claiborne who consents. Sur. Obadiah Winfree. Wit. George Reed. p. 91.

22 October 1804. William POINTER and Lucy Winfree, 21 years of age, dau. of James Winfree who consents. Sur. Major Winfree. William Pointer of Richmond City. p. 74.

10 September 1792. Zachariah POLLARD and Elizabeth Varner. Sur. George Pollard. Married 12 September by Rev. Needler Robinson, Rector of Dale Parish, Episcopal Church. p. 34.

13 December 1813. Caderick Petti POOL and Elizabeth Vaden, dau. of George Vaden, deceased. Sur. William Vaden. Married 22 December by Rev. Thomas Lafon, Church of Christ. p. 123.

15 February 1798. William POOL and Phebe Russell. Married by Rev. Benjamin Watkins. Ministers' Returns p. 387.

13 April 1810. William POOL and Susanna Jones, 21 years of age. Sur. William Nash. Wit. Edward Burnett and Archibald Shortt. p. 101.

9 July 1810. William POOL and Susanna Haskins. Sur. Edward Burnett. Wit. James Burnett. p. 103.

5 September 1801. Dutroy PORTER and Elizabeth Bell Bates, dau. of Eliza Bates who consents. Wit. John Porter and John Friend. This is consent only. Married 15 September by Rev. George Smith Baptist. p. 63.

18 December 1792. John PORTER and Polly Elam, dau. of Phebe Elam who consents. Wit. Richard Elam. This is consent only. See John Parter. p. 35.

2 October 1791. Stephen PORTER and _____ _____. Consent of Thomas Wooldridge for the bride. This is consent only. p. 33.

19 December 1798. Thomas PORTER and Catharine Cox, dau. of Henry Cox who consents. Sur. John Porter. Wit. Henry Cox, Jr. Married 29 December by Rev. Benjamin Watkins. p. 53.

17 January 1781. Aaron POWELL and Susan Taylor. Sur. Anthony Taylor. p. 14.

12 March 1798. Alexander POWELL and Nancy Powell, dau. of John and Sarah Powell who consent. Sur. Archibald Powell. Married 27 March by Rev. Benjamin Watkins. p. 51.

14 May 1798. Archibald POWELL and Elizabeth Welch, dau. of Mary Welch who consents. Sur. Alexander Powell. Married 26 May by Rev. Benjamin Watkins. p. 51.

23 May 1803. John POWELL and Sally Trent, dau. of John Trent who consents. Sur. Thomas Stanford. Married 26 May by Rev. Benjamin Watkins. p. 67.

13 January 1809. Jonathan POWELL and Hannah Trent, 21 years of age, dau. of John Trent. Sur. Jesse Taylor. p. 95.

9 March 1812. Joshua POWELL and Mary Bowles, dau. of John Bowles who consents. Sur. Langhorne Simpson. p. 113.

8 November 1802. William POWELL and Nancy Edwards, dau. of John Edwards who consents. Wit. William Edwards. p. 66.

9 December 1799. David PRICE and Cynthia Walthall, dau. of Eliza Walthall who consents. Wit. Marley Walthall. This is consent only. p. 56.

10 December 1810. Joseph PRICE and Nancy Ironmonger. Consent of Philip Turpin for nancy; no relationship stated. Sur. Allen McRae. Wit. V. Winfree. p. 105.

26 February 1814. John A. PRIDE and Martha Covington, 21 years of age. Sur. Robert V. Fagg. Wit. William Covington. p. 124.

4 April 1772. Peter PRIDE and Mary Dance. Sur. Edward Dance.
p. 1.

6 August 1795. Peter PRIDE and Rebecca Smith who signs her own
consent. Wit. James Pride. This is consent only. Married 8
August by Rev. Needler Robinson, Rector of Dale Parish, Episcopal
Church. p. 41.

23 October 1815. Thomas PRIDE and Mary L. Burton, dau. of
Richard Burton who consents and is surety. Married 9 November
by Rev. Joseph Gill, Jr. p. 131.

23 September 1812. John PRINGLE and Martha P. Sims, dau. of
James Sims who consents. Sur. John Sims. p. 116.

June 1787-June 1788. Archibald PUCKETT and Elizabeth Davis.
Married by Rev. Eleazer Clay, Baptist. Ministers' Returns p.
372.

1785-1786. Benjamin PUCKETT and Sarah Whitworth. Married by
Rev. Eleazer Clay, Baptist. Ministers' Returns p. 371.

8 October 1810. Benjamin PUCKETT and Sarah Fowler. Sur. Isham
Puckett. Married 10 October by Rev. Edmund Goode, Baptist.
p. 104.

21 December 1799. Carter PUCKETT and Phebe Cashon, dau. of
Burwell Cashon who consents. Sur. James Cashon. (I think this
name is Cashion.) Married by Rev. Eleazer Clay, Baptist. p. 57.

_____ 1792. Claiborne PUCKETT and Jane Blankenship.
Married by Rev. Eleazer Clay, Baptist. Ministers' Returns p.
379.

27 October 1814. Isham PUCKETT and Frances R. Baugh, dau. of
Jeremiah Baugh who consents. Sur. Robertson Baugh. p. 126.

23 December 1796. James PUCKETT and Rebecca Frifth. Sur.
Burwell Cashion. Married by Rev. Eleazer Clay, Baptist. p. 46.

24 October 1789. Joel PUCKETT and Sarah Jones. Married by Rev.
Richard Garrettson of the town of Petersburg. Ministers'
Returns p. 376.

2 August 1813. Levi PUCKETT and Elizabeth Patram, widow of John
Patram. Sur. Thomas Perdue. Married 12 August by Rev. Joseph
Gill, Jr. p. 121.

21 December 1803. Lewis PUCKETT and Rhody Newby, dau. of
Sarah Baugh who consents. Wit. Nathaniel Newby and John Smith.
John Puckett, father of Lewis, consents for him. p. 70.

_____ 1792. Lodwick PUCKETT and Kesiah Blankenship. Married by Rev. Eleazer Clay, Baptist. Ministers' Returns p. 379.

6 April 1781. Nathaniel PUCKETT and Mary Nunnally. Sur. James Patielo. Married 12 April by Rev. Eleazer Clay, Baptist. p. 1

5 April 1796. Rowland PUCKETT and Sarah Moxley. Sur. Enock Roberts. Married by Rev. Eleazer Clay, Baptist. p. 44.

1 March 1788. William PUCKETT and Pheby Perdue. Sur. Burwell Cashioñ. Married by Rev. Eleazer Clay, Baptist. p. 26.

23 May 1811. John PURDIE and Elizabeth Spears, dau. of John Spears who consents. Sur. Isham Cheatham. Wit. Absalom Baugh. p. 108.

18 December 1780. David PURKINSON and Mary Cobb. Sur. John Peery. See David Perkinson. p. 13.

4 August 1781. Ezekiel PURKINSON and Nanne Bragg, dau. of Hugh Bragg who consents. This is consent only. p. 14.

29 May 1807. John RAILEY and Elizabeth Railey, dau. of James Railey, deceased. Martin Railey, guardian of Elizabeth, consen for her and is surety. Married by Rev. Eleazar Clay, Baptist. p. 86.

11 January 1808. Harry RANDOLPH and Caroline Matilda Delia Smith, dau. of Obadiah Smith. Sur. John Friend. p. 89.

9 January 1808. Peter Beverley RANDOLPH and Lavania R. Heath, dau. of Harry Heath who consents. Sur. James Currie. Wit. Richard Randolph. p. 89.

4 May 1805. Richard Bland RANDOLPH and Jerusha Anderson, 21 years of age, dau. of Jerusha Anderson. Sur. William Anderson. p. 76.

8 April 1795. Thomas Eston RANDOLPH and Jane Randolph, sister of Thomas M. Randolph and H. Randolph who consent. Wit. D. M. Randolph. This is consent only. p. 41.

31 December 1781. Philip RATLIFFE and Anne Baugh, of lawful age. Sur. John Walthall. Wit. Mary Farmer and Elizabeth Burge. p. 15.

7 March 1772. Gwyn READ and Mary Folks. Sur. Edward Worsham. p. 1.

4 November 1805. John B. READ and Susanna Pride. James Pride, guardian of Susanna, consents for her. Sur. Thomas E. Gary. Wit. Daniel Boisseau. p. 79.

9 January 1782. Milner READ and Damaris Cox, dau. of Judith Cox. Sur. Milner Cox. p. 16.

28 June 1814. Daniel REAMS and Elizabeth Britton, dau. of William Britton who consents and is surety. p. 125.

20 June 1811. Erasmus REAMS and Elizabeth Cunningham. Sur. John Godsey. Married by Rev. Benjamin Watkins. p. 109.

22 July 1805. William REAMS and Mary Covington, 21 years of age, dau. of Francis Covington, deceased. Sur. William Edwards. p. 77.

12 August 1805. William REAVES and Mary Covington. Married by Rev. Henry Featherstone, Sr. Ministers' Returns p. 397.

3 December 1773. Henry REESE and Sally Smith. Sur. James Boisseau. p. 3.

31 May 1815. John RICHARD and Mary Ann Gibbs. Sur. Peter Gill. Wit. Matthew Gibbs. Married 3 June by Rev. Joseph Gill, Jr. p. 130.

5 March 1784. Thomas RICHARDS and Mrs. Martha Cuthell. This is consent only. p. 20.

26 December 1800. Enoch ROBERTS and Tabitha Wright. Sur. James Elam. Married by Rev. Eleazer Clay, Baptist. p. 61.

30 October 1780. Evan ROBERTS and Mary Smith. Sur. John Clayton. p. 12.

4 December 1815. Henry ROBERTS and Phaney Branch, dau. of Edward Branch, deceased. Sur. Daniel Cheatham. Married 7 December by Rev. Edmund Goode, Baptist. p. 132.

3 October 1810. Jacob ROBERTS and Elizabeth Markham, widow of Benjamin Markham. Sur. Benjamin Osborne. p. 104.

12 March 1798. Olive ROBERTS and Mary Brummall. Sur. Benjamin Brummall. p. 51.

13 March 1815. Richard ROBERTS and Pamela Baugh, dau. of John Baugh who consents. Sur. Abram S. Wooldridge. Married 16 March by Rev. Benjamin Watkins. p. 129.

10 July 1807. Thomas Baldwin ROBERTS and Lucy Flournoy, dau. of Jacob Flournoy who consents. Sur. Parke Poindexter. Wit. Phillip Vest and Mark Flournoy. p. 86.

11 October 1799. William ROBERTS and Martha Walthall. Married by Rev. Benjamin Watkins. Ministers' Returns p. 390.

7 January 1801. William ROBERTS and Levinia Chalkley, 22 years of age. Sign their own consent. Wit. Edward Hill and James Hill. This is consent only. Married by Rev. Eleazer Clay, Baptist. p. 62.

19 April 1793. Elijah ROBERTSON and Nancy Purdie, dau. of Aaron Purdie who consents. Sur. John Bass. Wit. Richard Mosley and Arthur Mosley. Married 24 April by Rev. James Rucks. p. 36.

17 December 1811. Field ROBERTSON and Lucy Worsham, dau. of Michael Worsham who consents. Sur. Edward Worsham. Wit. Polly Vaden and Prudence Worsham. p. 111.

29 June 1787. Isaac ROBERTSON and Mary Short. Married by Rev. William Webber, Baptist. Ministers' Returns p. 371.

21 July 1782. James ROBERTSON and Susanna More. Married by Rev. William Hickman, Minister of Skinquarter Baptist Church. Ministers' Returns p. 369.

18 August 1788. James ROBERTSON and Martha Field Archer. John Archer, executor, consents for Martha. No relationship stated. This is consent only. p. 27.

12 November 1798. James ROBERTSON and Nancy Sims. Wit. Charles Elam. This is consent only. Married 17 November by Rev. Nathan Anderson, Methodist. p. 53.

14 April 1806. John ROBERTSON and Catharine Traylor, dau. of Archibald Traylor, Sr. who consents and is surety. Married by Rev. Thomas Lafon, Church of Christ. p. 81.

25 August 1806. John F. ROBERTSON and Mary C. Gordon, 21 years of age. Sur. James Gordon. Wit. Ann Bludes. p. 82.

24 April 1798. Jonas Robertson and Catherine Markham. Married by Rev. Nathan Anderson, Methodist. Ministers' Returns p. 388.

28 February 1805. Joseph Warren ROBERTSON and Judith Branch, 21 years of age. Sur. Charles Burton. p. 75.

6 April 1808. Joseph Roy ROBERTSON and Lucy Brooks. Sur. James Brooks. Joseph Roy son of John Robertson of Amelia County, who consents for him. p. 90.

12 November 1792. Moses ROBERTSON and Jamima Nunnally. Wit. Charles Hamlin and Herod Vaden. This is consent only. Married 25 November by Rev. Needler Robinson, Rector of Dale Parish, Episcopal Church. p. 34.

_____ 1787. Walthall ROBERTSON and Frances Cox. Married by Rev. John Goode. Ministers' Returns p. 372.

18 October 1794. Walthall ROBERTSON and Ann Cary. Married by Rev. Benjamin Watkins. Ministers' Returns p. 382.

2 November 1797. William ROBERTSON and Judith Bass. Married by Rev. Nathan Anderson, Methodist. Ministers' Returns p. 385.

15 December 1808. Robert ROBINSON and Anne Archer, dau. of John Archer, deceased. Sur. Richard Finch. p. 94.

26 July 1804. Charles ROCKE and Polly Archer, dau. of Elizabeth Archer who consents. Sur. Alexander Marshall. p. 72.

3 April 1796. Joseph ROGERS and Nancy Hardin. Daniel Boisseau, guardian of Nancy, consents for her. Sur. William Perkinson. Wit. Thomas Branch and John Pride. p. 43.

6 January 1807. John ROPER and Asenath Hatcher, dau. of Nathaniel Hatcher, deceased. Sur. Obed Hatcher. Wit. Little-berry Taylor. John son of Samuel Roper. p. 85.

12 November 1801. Joseph ROPER and Martha Elam. Married by Rev. George Smith, Baptist. Ministers' Returns p. 394.

23 August 1813. Howell ROSE and Maria M. Bryant "who has lived at Capt. Edmund Locketts for 7 years." Dau. of William G. Bryant. Sur. Francis Watkins. Wit. Edmund Lockett and Mary E. Logwood. p. 121.

4 May 1785. William ROSS and Elizabeth Hix. Sur. John Minton. p. 23.

7 March 1804. Daniel ROWLETT and Rebecca Patram, dau. of Francis Patram who consents. Sur. William Patram. Wit. William Talbott. p. 71.

16 March 1808. Daniel ROWLETT and Lucy Worsham, dau. of Mary
Patram who consents. Sur. Bevill Archer. Wit. Daniel Patram.
p. 90.

5 February 1779. George ROWLETT and Patty Moseley. Sur. Daniel
Patram. p. 8.

25 December 1783. John ROWLETT and Martha Covington, dau. of
Richard Covington who consents. Sur. Thomas Covington. p. 20.

___ January 1789. John ROWLETT and Mary Dance. Married by Rev.
John Cameron, Rector of Bristol Parish, Episcopal Church.

23 April 1791. John ROWLETT and Locky Brown. Married by Rev.
John Cameron, Rector of Bristol Parish, Episcopal Church.

19 May 1806. John ROWLETT and Lucy Patram, dau. of Francis
Patram, Sr. who consents. Sur. William Patram. Wit. Isham
Graves and William Talbott. p. 81.

3 February 1778. Peter ROWLETT and Sarah Lester. Sur. Henry
Meideras. p. 6.

_____ 1788. Peter ROWLETT and Sarah Stringer. Married by
Rev. John Goode. Ministers' Returns p. 373.

27 June 1797. Thomas ROWLETT and Elizabeth Farmer. Sur. Franci
Dunnivant. Married by Rev. Eleazer Clay, Baptist. p. 48.

12 April 1813. Thomas ROWLETT and ____ ____. Sur. Thomas
Pride. p. 120.

4 March 1785. William ROWLETT and Elizabeth Gill, dau. of James
Gill who consents. Sur. William Clarke. p. 22.

6 February 1795. William ROWLETT and Mary Stringer. Sur. John
Wilkerson. Married 12 February by Rev. Thomas Hardie, Methodist
p. 40.

22 December 1807. William ROWLETT and Polly Gill, 21 years of
age, dau. of Daniel Gill, deceased. Sur. John Rowlett. p. 88.

24 December 1809. William ROWLETT, Jr. and Betsey Rowlett, dau.
of John Rowlett, Sr., who consents. Sur. John Rowlett, Jr.
Wit. George Rowlett. p. 99.

4 February 1777. John ROYALL and Judith Perkinson. Sur. William Perkinson. See John Ryal. p. 5.

15 December 1810. Richard ROYALL and Mary Block, widow of Thomas Block. Sur. Joseph Dillion. p. 106.

21 December 1809. Robert ROYALL and Rebecca Akin, dau. of Thomas Akin who consents. Sur. Chambling Batte. p. 99.

11 June 1810. Hardiman ROYSTER and Jane Ronald. William Fenwick, guardian of Jane, consents for her. Sur. Nicholas Mills. Wit. John Ashton. p. 102.

12 September 1806. John ROZELL and Polly Green Baker, dau. of James Herndon who is surety. Wit. William S. Dance. This must mean step-daughter. p. 82.

21 May 1780. Jacob RUBSAMEN and Lucy Bland. Sur. Thomas Goode. p. 11.

12 March 1793. James RUCKS and Sarah Moseley. Sur. Leonard Cheatham. p. 20.

4 November 1801. Elijah RUDD and Sally Robertson, dau. of Martha Goode who consents. Sur. William Pinchback. Married by Rev. Charles Forsee, Minister of Skinquarter Baptist Church. p. 64.

27 December 1806. Frederick RUDD and Salley Rudd. Married by Rev. Charles Forsee, Skinquarter Baptist Church. Ministers' Returns p. 400.

30 November 1778. James RUDD and Ann Cheatham. Sur. Bernard Cheatham. p. 7.

18 September 1789. John RUDD and Sinai Clarke, dau. of Jesse Clarke who consents. Sur. Thomas Talbott. Married by Rev. Eleazer Clay, Baptist. p. 28.

24 May 1806. John RUDD and Senir Rudd. Married by Rev. Charles Forsee, Skinquarter Baptist Church. Ministers' Returns p. 400.

23 October 1811. John RUDD and Oney Rudd. Sur. Frederick Rudd. p. 110.

22 May 1810. Leonard RUDD and Winefred Covington Beasley, 21 years of age, dau. of Henry Beasley, deceased. Sur. William Beasley. Married 9 June by Rev. Edmund Goode, Baptist. p. 102.

9 May 1814. Robert RUDD and Polly Berks. Jeremiah Nunnally guardian of Polly consents for her. Sur. John Goode. Wit. Edward Goode. Married by Rev. Edmund Goode, Baptist. p. 125.

24 October 1793. Hezekiah RUSSELL and Rhoda Blankenship. Married by Rev. James Rucks. Ministers' Returns p. 381.

7 July 1794. Jeremiah RUSSELL and Vina Blankenship. Sur. John Condrey. Married 10 July by Rev. James Rucks. p. 39.

3 April 1803. Jesse RUSSELL and Elizabeth Condry. Married by Rev. Charles Forsee, Minister of Skinquarter Baptist Church. Ministers' Returns p. 393.

24 October 1793. John RUSSELL and Anna Clay. Sur. William Winfree. p. 37.

21 August 1798. John RUSSELL and Ann Akin. Married by Rev. Nathan Anderson, Methodist. Ministers' Returns p. 388.

3 March 1800. John Northcut RUSSEL and Patty Moore. Sur. Jeremiah Russel. Wit. Page P. Finney. p. 60.

5 January 1809. Peter F. RUSSELL and Appy Fargusson, 21 years of age, dau. of Aaron Fargusson. Sur. Martin Davis. Wit. Mose Fargusson and Haily Fargusson. p. 95.

10 February 1799. Royal RUSSELL and Patsey Clark. Sur. Reuben Short. Wit. Jesse Clarke and William Goodger. Married 23 February by Rev. Benjamin Watkins. p. 54.

1801-1802. Thomas RUSSELL and Elizabeth Lester. Married by Re Eleazar Clay, Baptist. Ministers' Returns p. 394.

4 February 1777. John RYAL and Judith Perkinson. Sur. William Perkinson. See John Royall. p. 5.

9 February 1778. Thomas SADLER and Hannah Hamlin. Sur. Peter Talbot. p. 6.

12 March 1796. John SALLEE' and Mary Smith. Mary signs her ow consent. Wit. William Fowler. This is consent only. p. 43.

29 May 1815. Thomas SALMON and Elizabeth Worsham. Sur. Richar Royall. Married 1 June by Rev. Thomas Lafon, Church of Christ. p. 130.

21 February 1794. William SASSEEN and Sally Roper, dau. of Joseph Roper who consents. Wit. William Smith. This is consent only. Married by Rev. James Smith of Powhatan County. p. 38.

19 December 1812. Robert SAUNDERS and Martha F. Harris. Robert Harris, guardian of Martha, consents for her. Sur. David Morrissett. Wit. Edward Wooldridge. p. 118.

14 December 1807. Tarleton SAUNDERS and Salley B. Lyle, widow of James Lyle, Jr. Sur. Robert Graham. Wit. Sarah H. Goode. p. 88.

20 November 1800. Andrew SCOTT and Phebe Flournoy. Married by Rev. Benjamin Watkins. Ministers' Returns p. 393.

17 March 1796. James SCOTT and Margaret Booker. Married by Rev. Needler Robinson, Rector of Dale Parish, Episcopal Church. Ministers' Returns p. 378.

9 July 1804. James SCOTT and Martha Goode, dau. of Robert Goode who consents. Sur. George (illegible). p. 72.

27 September 1811. Thomas SCOTT and Mary Tisdale. Sur. William Clarke. "Neighbor and relation to both." p. 110.

20 May 1784. William SCOTT and Elizabeth Wade. Sur. Thomas Howlett. p. 21.

21 September 1797. Thomas SCRUGGS and Jane Scott. Sur. Andrew Scott. Wit. William Finney. Married 23 September by Rev. Benjamin Watkins. p. 48.

1 April 1805. James SELBY and Nancy Gill, dau. of Joseph Gill who consents and is surety. Married by Rev. Eleazar Clay, Baptist. p. 76.

12 October 1772. William SHACKLETON and Mary Hopkins. Sur. Solomon Gordon. p. 2.

June 1787-June 1788. John SHADDOIN and Sarah Wilkinson. Married by Rev. Eleazer Clay, Baptist. Ministers' Returns p. 372.

11 August 1806. Colin SHEFFIELD and Elizabeth Michaels, dau. of John Michaels, deceased. Sur. Peter Sheffield. p. 82.

3 December 1779. John SHELL and Margaret Smith, dau. of William Smith. Sur. H. Archer. p. 10.

17 August 1811. Thomas SHELL and Frances Nunnally, 21 years of age, dau. of Daniel Nunnally. Sur. James Hall. p. 109.

26 October 1795. William SHIELDS and Mary Barker. Sur. Jones Allen. Wit. Thomas Finney. p. 42.

6 April 1802. John SHIPWASH and Judea Short, dau. of Ann Short who consents. Wit. James Foster. p. 65.

26 February 1806. Malone SHOEMAKER and Sidnew Pritchard. Sur. Richard Pritchard. p. 81.

23 August 1814. Archibald SHORT and Sarah Brooks, dau. of Elias Brooks who consents. Sur. Archer Farmer. Wit. David Wells and Fanny Farmer. Married 24 August by Rev. Thomas Lafon, Church of Christ. p. 125.

14 October 1802. John SHORT and Nancy Hubbard. Married by Rev. Benjamin Watkins. Ministers' Returns p. 396.

2 September 1812. Samuel SHORT and Rebecca Edwards, dau. of John Edwards who consents. Sur. Edmund Wells. Wit. Lewis Thompson. Married 3 September by Rev. John Potts. p. 116.

13 January 1796. William SHORT and Susannah Crump, dau. of Jesse Crump who consents. Sur. Jesse Chapple. Married 20 January by Rev. Benjamin Watkins. p. 43.

23 July 1804. William SHORT and Patsey Gardner, widow of Henry Gardner. Sur. William Shortt. p. 72.

23 August 1814. William SHORT and Martha Walden, dau. of Matthew and Elizabeth Walden who consent. Sur. John Walden. Wit. Mary Walden and Esther Walden. p. 126.

4 November 1799. Young William SHORT and Polly Lester. Sur. Allyson Clarke. Married by Rev. Eleazer Clay, Baptist. p. 56 says Young W.; p. 485 says Young William. p. 56.

20 April 1811. Obadiah SHORTT and Elizabeth Shortt, dau. of William Shortt who consents. Sur. Richard Branch. Wit. Archer Farmer, William Short, Jr. and Rachel Gardner. p. 108.

31 May 1811. Carrington SIMPSON and Disey Powell. Sur. Jesse Taylor. p. 109.

12 April 1802. John SIMPSON and Elizabeth B. Pride. Hill
Cogbill, guardian of Elizabeth, consents for her. Wit. David
Patterson, Jr. Married 17 April by Rev. Needler Robinson, Rector
of Dale Parish, Episcopal Church who says Elizabeth B. Pride.
p. 65.

18 December 1805. John SIMPSON and Phebe Flournoy, 21 years of
age. Sur. Lawrence Flournoy. Married by Rev. Benjamin Watkins
who dates his return 3 January 1806. p. 79.

29 September 1806. Langhorne SIMPSON and Elizabeth Godsey, dau.
of John Godsey, Sr. who consents. Sur. John Godsey, Jr. Wit.
Solomon Godsey. p. 82.

_____ 1788. James SIMS and Martha Binns. Married by Rev.
John Goode. Ministers' Returns p. 373.

18 January 1804. John SIMS and Tabitha Rudd. Sur. Hezekiah
Rudd. p. 70.

22 April 1798. William SIMS and Susannah Boles. Sur. Charles
Elam. Married 25 April by Rev. Nathan Anderson, Methodist.
p. 51.

15 May 1809. Richard SIZER and Maria Simpson, 21 years of age,
grand dau. of Josiah Flournoy. Sur. John Simpson. p. 97.

9 July 1809. Samuel SIZER and Nancy Flournoy, 21 years of age,
dau. of Jacob Flournoy, deceased. Sur. Samuel Flournoy. p. 97.

6 April 1805. Alexander Smith and Patience Turner, dau. of
William Turner. Sur. Stephen Turner. p. 76.

21 January 1779. Benjamin SMITH and Sarah Owen. Sur. Charles
Hundley. p. 8.

29 August 1811. Benjamin B. SMITH and Charity Smith, dau. of
William Smith who consents. Sur. Richard Smith. p. 109.

9 April 1811. Beverly SMITH and Ann B. Beverly. Sur. Peter
F. Smith. p. 108.

29 March 1789. Charles SMITH and Mary Wilson. Married by Rev.
Needler Robinson, Rector of Dale Parish, Episcopal Church.
Ministers' Returns p. 374.

7 March 1775. Clayton SMITH and Sarah Grizel, dau. of William
Grizel. Sur. George Grizel. Wit. John Caldwell. p. 4.

9 July 1810. Jabez SMITH and Mary L. Walthall. Sur. Samuel Ha
Married 14 July by Rev. John Cox of Petersburg, Methodist.
p. 103.

10 April 1815. James SMITH and Elizabeth Wyatt, 21 years of age
Levinia Perdue (sister) consents for Elizabeth. Sur. John
Wyatt. Married 12 April by Rev. Joseph Gill, Jr. p. 129.

10 October 1787. Jesse SMITH and Martha Keys. Married by Rev.
John Cameron, Rector of Bristol Parish, Episcopal Church.

3 September 1788. John SMITH and Rebecca Cogbill, dau. of
William Cogbill who consents. This is consent only. Married
5 September by Rev. Needler Robinson, Rector of Dale Parish.
Episcopal Church. p. 27.

19 May 1790. John SMITH and Fanny Clayton. Married by Rev.
Needler Robinson, Rector of Dale Parish, Episcopal Church.
Ministers' Returns p. 375.

   September 1790. John SMITH and Sally Dyson. Married by Rev.
John Cameron, Rector of Bristol Parish, Episcopal Church.

14 January 1793. John SMITH and Ann Chalkley. Married by Rev.
Needler Robinson, Rector of Dale Parish, Episcopal Church.
Ministers' Returns p. 377.

14 December 1812. John SMITH and Sally Male, 21 years of age.
Sur. William Vaden. p. 118.

29 December 1785. Jory SMITH and Sarah Clayton. Married by
Rev. William Leigh, Rector of Manchester Parish, Episcopal
Church. Ministers' Returns p. 370.

4 August 1780. Joseph SMITH and ____ _____. Sur. James Elam.
p. 12.

23 March 1804. Lindsay SMITH and Phebe Norrice. Sur. Jory
Smith. Wit. Sarah Smith. Married 24 March by Rev. Henry
Featherstone, Sr. p. 71.

9 February 1786. Ric(hard) SMITH and Susanna Irwin, dau. of
Thomas William Irwin who consents. This is consent only. p. 24

12 April 1800. Richard SMITH and Polly Brittain. Married by
Rev. Needler Robinson, Rector of Dale Parish, Episcopal Church.
Ministers' Returns p. 390.

2 September 1807. Robert SMITH and Dolley French. Sur. Jeremiah Ligon. Wit. Tarleton Saunders. p. 87.

23 December 1811. Thomas SMITH and Elizabeth Saseen. Sur. William Smith. p. 111.

1 March 1779. William SMITH and Mary Cacey. Sur. Guliemus Wood. p. 9.

26 November 1791. William SMITH and Mary Farlager. Married by Rev. Needler Robinson, Rector of Dale Parish, Episcopal Church. Ministers' Returns p. 377.

11 November 1805. William SMITH and Sarah Womack, 22 years of age, dau. of William Womack, deceased. Sur. William Dillion. Wit. William S. Dance. Married 21 November by Rev. Henry Featherstone, Sr. p. 79.

23 March 1813. William SMITH and Lucy Anthony, 21 years of age. Sur. John Smith. Married 25 March by Rev. Joseph Gill, Jr. p. 119.

27 October 1807. Alexander SNELLINGS and Virginia Mann, dau. of Branch Mann who consents. Sur. Martin Brooks. Wit. George Snellings, Baker Mann, Thomas Perdue and Lucretia Perdue. p. 87.

_____ _____ 1792. George SNELLINGS and Winney Mann, dau. of Branch Mann who consents. Wit. Armstead Graves. Married by Rev. Eleazar Clay, Baptist. p. 497.

22 April 1809. George SNELLINGS and Barbara Roberts, dau. of Enock Roberts, Sr. who consents. Sur. Enock Roberts. Wit. Tabitha Roberts and Isham Puckett. p. 97.

1 September 1785. James SNELLINGS and Mimy Fargerson, dau. of Aaron Fargesson who consents. Sur. Daniel Vaden. Married 8 October by Rev. William Leigh, Rector of Manchester Parish, Episcopal Church. He says Mima Ferguson. p. 23.

1797-1799. Jesse SNELLINGS and Rebecca Brooks. Married by Rev. Eleazer Clay, Baptist. Ministers' Returns p. 392.

24 January 1798. John SNELLINGS and Tabitha Flournoy, dau. of Josiah Flournoy who consents. Sur. Samuel Flournoy. Wit. Ann Flournoy. Married 26 January by Rev. Benjamin Watkins. p. 50.

9 January 1809. John SNELLINGS and Polly Elam, dau. of Richard Elam who consents. Sur. Samuel Flournoy. Wit. Phebe Flournoy. p. 95.

1 January 1810. Thomas SNELLINGS and Sarah Wood, 21 years of age, dau. of Gulielmus Wood. Sur. Joseph Wood. p. 100.

5 February 1779. Lewis SOUBLET and Mary Trabue. Sur. Joseph Watkins. See Lewis Sublet. p. 8.

25 December 1798. James SOUTHALL and Judith Wilkinson. Married by Rev. Nathan Anderson, Methodist. Ministers' Returns p. 388.

3 December 1807. George SOWELL and Susanna Cox, 21 years of age dau. of John Cox, deceased. Sur. Henry Cox. Wit. Marly Cox. p. 88.

13 August 1807. Richard SPAIN and Lucy Johnson, dau. of David Johnson. Sur. John Dishman. Married 15 August by Rev. John Cox Methodist. p. 86.

_____ _____ 1787. John SPEARS and Mary Hill. Married by Rev. John Goode. Ministers' Returns p. 373.

9 April 1804. John SPEARS and Susanna Womack. Sur. Peter Rowlett. p. 71.

24 January 1797. Hickman SPILLAR and Catherine M. Smith, dau. of Francis Smith who consents. Wit. Rebecca Smith and Francis Smith, Jr. p. 46.

5 October 1795. John SPOTSWOOD and Mary Goode, dau. of Robert Goode who consents. This is consent only. p. 42.

31 March 1803. Robert SPOTSWOOD and Louisa Batte. Married by Rev. Needler Robinson, Rector of Dale Parish, Episcopal Church. Ministers' Returns p. 391.

21 May 1811. Rowland SPROUSE and Martha Gibson, dau. of John Gibson of Buckingham County. Sur. John Vest. Wit. Joseph Bening. Martha is living in Chesterfield with her sister, Betsy Vest. p. 108.

30 July 1794. James STAFFORD and Polly Wilson. Sur. Josiah Dunnavant. Wit. Stephen Gill. Married by Rev. Eleazer Clay, Baptist. p. 39.

18 December 1797. Beverley STANARD and Jane W. Fleming, dau. of William Fleming who consents. Wit. Edward Moseley and John Markham. This is consent only. p. 49.

6 February 1798. Beverley Chew STANARD and Mary Bolling Fleming dau. of William Fleming who consents. Sur. Beverly Stanard. Wit. Erasmus Reams. p. 50.

7 April 1813. Beverley C(hew) STANARD and Eliza M. Watts. Sur.
David Weisiger. Wit. Seigniora T. Smith. p. 119.

3 July 1798. Thomas STANDFORD and Sallee Wooldridge, dau. of
Edward Wooldridge who consents. Wit. Cornelius Ellett. This is
consent only. Married 7 July by Rev. Benjamin Watkins. p. 52.

14 January 1809. Moses STANDLEY and Jane Dunlavy, widow of
Anthony Dunlavy. Sur. Henry Walthall, Jr. Wit. Lawson
Dunnington. p. 95.

_____ _____ 1791. David STANFORD and Sarah Godsey. Married by
Rev. James Smith. Return dated 10 March 1791, Manakin Town.
Ministers' Returns p. 377.

22 December 1780. Robert STEPHEN and Elizabeth Farmer. Sur.
John Crisp. p. 13.

_____ _____ 1788. Robert STEPHENS and Sarah Farmer. Married by
Rev. John Goode. Ministers' Returns p. 373.

June 1787-June 1788. Robert STEPHENS and Mary Turner. Married
by Rev. Eleazer Clay, Baptist. Ministers' Returns p. 372.

7 December 1814. William STEPHENSON and Malinda Goode, dau. of
Richard Goode who consents. Sur. David Goode. Wit. Jesse
Brooks. Married by Rev. Thomas Lafon, Church of Christ. p.
127.

23 December 1777. James STEUART and Suckey Steuart. Sur.
Repto Steuart. p. 5.

13 December 1808. Jerrard STEWARD and Betsey Harris, dau. of
Edward Harris who consents and is surety. p. 94.

6 August 1806. John STEWART and Jane Farmer, dau. of Samuel
Farmer who consents and is surety. Married 8 August by Rev.
Henry Featherstone, Sr. p. 82.

19 April 1815. Josiah STEWART and Rebecca Gates, dau. of
Richard Gates who consents and is surety. Married 20 April by
Rev. Edmund Goode. p. 129.

12 December 1814. William STEWART and Cynthia Farmer. Sur.
Samuel Farmer. Married 19 December by Rev. Thomas Lafon,
Church of Christ. p. 127.

13 February 1788. Jesse STILES and Sarah Potter. Married by
Rev. John Cameron, Rector of Bristol Parish, Episcopal Church.

28 October 1796. James R. STOKES and Nancy Short. Sur. Young William Short. p. 45.

19 February 1789. Daniel STONE and Anna Beasley. Consent of Samuel Hatcher, guardian. (Of which one?) Married 7 March by Rev. Needler Robinson, Rector of Dale Parish, Episcopal Church. p. 27.

15 December 1779. William STONE and Martha Worsham. Consent of John Cayse, father of Martha. Does this mean step-father? Sur. George Grissell. p. 10.

12 March 1813. Theophilus F. STRACHAN and Jane H. Stratton, dau. of John Stratton who consents. Sur. John F. May. p. 119.

4 August 1780. Henry STRATTON and Anne Bass. Sur. George Markham. p. 12.

3 January 1783. Henry STRATTON and _____ _____. Sur. George Markham. p. 17.

13 June 1789. John STRATTON and Dorothy Batte. Married by Rev. Needler Robinson, Rector of Dale Parish, Episcopal Church. Ministers' Returns p. 374.

27 December 1806. David STREET and Frances S. Trabue, dau. of William Trabue who consents. Sur. J. W. Webber. p. 84.

20 February 1815. David STREET and Polley Cole, dau. of John Cole who consents. Sur. John Cole, Jr. p. 128.

14 August 1815. James C. STRINGER and Hannah Rowlett, dau. of Peter Rowlett. Sur. Lee Roy Hall. Married 17 August by Rev. Thomas Anderson, Sr. p. 131.

_____ _____ 1788. William STRINGER and Sarah Williams. Married by Rev. John Goode. Ministers' Returns p. 373.

20 November 1801. Nathaniel STURD and Lusey Barber. Married by Rev. Henry Featherstone, Sr. Ministers' Returns p. 392.

13 April 1805. Henry STURDIVANT and Frances Crawley. Sur. Richard Gregory. Wit. Peter Franklin. Married 14 April by Rev. Henry Featherstone, Sr. p. 76.

11 July 1789. John STYLES and Susanna Nunnally. Married by Rev. Needler Robinson, Rector of Dale Parish, Episcopal Church. Ministers' Returns p. 374.

5 February 1779. Lewis SUBLETT and Mary Trabue. Sur. Joseph Watkins. See Lewis Soublet. p. 8.

12 October 1808. Peter SUBLETT and Anne P. Baker, dau. of Thomas Baker, Sr. who consents. Sur. Josiah Ellett. Peter Sublett of Powhatan County. p. 93.

_____ 1791. Moses SYRA and Elizabeth Roberts. Married by Rev. James Smith. Return dated 10 March 1791, Manakin Town. Ministers' Returns p. 377.

_____ 1792. Bartholomew SYRE and Sarah Baugh. Married by Rev. Eleazer Clay, Baptist. Ministers' Returns p. 379.

_____ 1790. Thomas TALBOTT and Phebe Clarke. Married by Rev. Eleazer Clay, Baptist. Ministers' Returns p. 376.

__ January 1800. William TALBOTT and Elizabeth Patram. Sur. Peter Worsham. Wit. John Cary and Page P. Finney. p. 59.

23 January 1802. Zachary TATUM and Obedience Beasley. This is consent only. p. 64.

27 May 1808. Arbin TAYLOR and Polly Perkinson, 21 years of age, dau. of William Perkinson, deceased. Sur. Francis R. Gibbs. Wit. Bolling Male. Married 3 June by Rev. John Cox, Methodist. Double wedding! See William Noble. p. 91.

20 April 1810. Daniel TAYLOR and Patsey H. Hubbard, 21 years of age. Sur. James Stanford. Wit. Littleberry Taylor and William Short. p. 101.

6 September 1808. John B. TAYLOR and Rebecca Hix, dau. of William Hix who consents. Sur. Richard Walthall. Wit. Jesse Snellings. Married by Rev. Eleazar Clay, Baptist. p. 92.

23 December 1808. John TAYLOR and Polly Lockett, 21 years of age, dau. of Charles Lockett, deceased. Sur. Charles Lockett, Jr. p. 94.

23 February 1797. Littleberry TAYLOR and Sarah Roper, dau. of Samuel Roper who consents. Sur. Thomas Standford. p. 40.

1785-1786. Richard Crittenden TAYLOR and Mary Bowman. Married by Rev. Eleazer Clay, Baptist. Ministers' Returns p. 371.

30 July 1787. Richard TAYLOR and Sarah Flournoy. Sur. John Flournoy. Married by Rev. John Goode. p. 26.

28 December 1797. Richard TAYLOR and Elizabeth Taylor. Married by Rev. Thomas Hardie, Methodist. Ministers' Returns p. 389.

20 February 1809. Richard TAYLOR and Lucy Goodrich, widow of John Goodrich. Sur. John Moody. p. 96.

8 May 1810. Richard TAYLOR and Frances Sturdivant, widow of Henry Sturdivant. Sur. Peyton Fuqua. p. 102.

1 June 1801. Samuel TAYLOR and Amey Horner. Sur. James Ferguso Wit. J. Clay. Married by Rev. Eleazer Clay, Baptist. p. 63.

21 May 1811. Samuel TAYLOR, Jr. and Emely Fowler. Sur. Richard B. Goode. p. 108.

9 November 1788. Dr. Thomas Augustus TAYLOR and Martha Osborne. Edward Friend, uncle of Martha and executor of estate, consents for her. This is consent only. Married 30 November by Rev. Needler Robinson, Rector of Dale Parish, Episcopal Church. p. 27.

22 October 1799. Thomas A. TAYLOR and Ann Donald. Sur. Daniel Beasley. Married 27 October by Rev. Needler Robinson, Rector of Dale Parish, Episcopal Church. p. 56.

18 February 1807. Vincent TAYLOR and Frances C. Bowman, dau. of Pleasant Bowman. Sur. Granville Bowman. p. 85.

7 November 1789. William TAYLOR and Mary Stanford, dau. of David Stanford who consents. This is consent only. p. 29.

28 December 1791. Samuel TEMPLE and Molly Bass, dau. of Henry Bass who consents. This is consent only. p. 33.

2 August 1784. Thomas THAIT and Mary Sheppard. Sur. John Hancock. p. 21.

21 December 1805. Christopher THOMAS and Nancy Baker, dau. of John Baker who consents. Sur. Matthew Baker. Wit. Judith Gordon. p. 80.

15 March 1811. Robert THOMAS and Mary Green Booker Hatcher. Sur. George Cogbill. p. 107.

26 March 1801. John THOMPSON and Nelly Conner, dau. of Catherin Conner who consents. Sur. Anthony Blackburn. Wit. James Tomson p. 62.

9 September 1805. George W. THORNTON and Mary Randolph, dau. of Lucy Randolph who consents. Sur. Richard B. Goode. p. 78.

14 April 1813. Hezekiah THURMAN and Nancy McGruder, dau. of Zepheniah McGruder. Sur. Wade Sublett McGruder. Wit. Daniel Taylor. p. 120.

5 June 1780. Pleasant THURMAN and Magdalene Ammonett. Sur. John Thurman. She was a dau. of Andrew and Jean (Morriset) Ammonett and grand dau. of Jacob Ammonett. p. 12.

16 November 1809. Richard N. THWEATT and Polly Eppes, dau. of Francis Eppes, deceased. Sur. Parke Poindexter. p. 99.

14 December 1812. Thomas B. THWEATT and Nancy J. Wooldridge, dau. of Daniel Wooldridge who consents. Sur. Thomas Watkins, Jr. Married 16 December by Rev. Thomas Anderson. p. 117.

23 March 1813. William TICEHURST and Virginia Jones. Sur. Samuel Short. Wit. William Rowlett. p. 119.

2 July 1792. Jesse TILLERSON and Rebecka Blankenship, dau. of Mary Blankenship who consents. This is consent only. See Jesse Tillotson. p. 34.

_____ 1788. William TILLERSON and Elizabeth Blankenship. Married by Rev. John Goode. Ministers' Returns p. 373.

2 July 1792. Jesse TILLOTSON and Rebecca Blankenship, dau. of Mary Blankenship who consents. This is consent only. See Jesse Tillerson. p. 34.

5 September 1782. Thomas TOOMBS and Jean Gates. Married by Rev. William Hickman, Minister of Skinquarter Baptist Church. Ministers' Returns p. 369.

7 November 1811. Abner TOTTY and Edith Patram. James Moody consents for Edith; no relationship stated. Sur. John H. Archer. Married 9 November by Rev. Joseph Gill. p. 110.

20 March 1788. Benjamin TOTTY and Mary Blankenship. Married by Rev. John Cameron, Rector of Bristol Parish, Episcopal Church.

24 December 1802. B____ TOTTY and Nancy Cousins. Married by Rev. Henry Featherstone, Sr. Ministers' Returns p. 396.

6 April 1787.   Daniel TOTTY and Betsy Andrews.   Sur. Henry Dance.   p. 26.

10 March 1792.   Edward TOTTY and Agness Dance.   Married by Rev. Needler Robinson, Rector of Dale Parish, Episcopal Church. Ministers' Returns p. 377.

_____ _____ 1792.   Jesse TOTTY and Nancy Fowler.   Married by Re Eleazer Clay, Baptist.   Ministers' Returns p. 380.

5 January 1793.   Robert TOTTY and Sandal Andrews.   Sur. Daniel Totty.   Married 10 January by Rev. John Cameron, Rector of Bristol Parish, Episcopal Church.   p. 36.

8 February 1810.   Thomas TOTTY and Frances Philips, dau. of Anderson Philips who consents and is surety.   p. 100.

24 November 1789.   William TOTTY and Edith Andrews.   Sur. Thoma Worsham.   Wit. Philip Thweat.   Married 26 November by Rev. Needler Robinson, Rector of Dale Parish, Episcopal Church.   p. 29.

1801-1802.   Elisha TOWLER and Fatey Perdue.   Married by Rev. Eleazar Clay, Baptist.   Ministers' Returns p. 394.

2 March 1782.   Luke TOWLER and Sally Adkins.   Sur. George Markh p. 16.

1 July 1782.   Daniel TRABUE and Mary Haskins.   Sur. Robert Haskins.   Daniel b. 31 Mar. 1760 son of John James Trabue and Olymphia Dupuy.   p. 16.

17 August 1786.   Edward TRABUE and Martha Haskins.   Married by Rev. John Goode.   Edward Trabue son of John James and Olymphia (Dupuy) Trabue.   Ministers' Returns p. 371.

19 October 1797.   Edward TRABUE and Jane Clay, dau. of Eleazer Clay who consents.   This is consent only.   Married by Rev. Benjamin Watkins.   Edward Trabue son of John James and Olymphia (Dupuy) Trabue.   p. 49.

June 1788-June 1789.   Stephen TRABUE and Jane Haskins.   Married by Rev. Eleazer Clay, Baptist.   Stephen Trabue was son of John James and Olymphia (Dupuy) Trabue and grand son of Anthony Trabue.   Ministers' Returns p. 373.

3 February 1783.   William TRABUE and Elizabeth Haskins, dau. of Robert Haskins who consents.   This is consent only.   William so of John James Trabue and Olymphia Dupuy.   p. 17.

10 September 1804. William TRABUE and Polly Bass, widow. Sur. Royall Martin. Married 12 September by Rev. Benjamin Watkins. p. 73.

4 February 1793. Myal TRAYLER and Phebe Fowler. Josiah Fowler consents for Phebe. No relationship stated. Wit. Thomas Fowler. This is consent only. Married by Rev. Eleazer Clay, Baptist, who says Miel Traylor. p. 36.

25 January 1779. Archer TRAYLOR and Judith Markham. Sur. George Markham. p. 8.

_____ 1796. Archer TRAYLER and Ann Stringer. Married by Rev. Eleazer Clay, Baptist. Ministers' Returns p. 384.

17 December 1801. Archer TRAYLOR and Polly Davis. Married by Rev. Thomas Hardie, Methodist. Ministers' Returns p. 395.

13 February 1811. Arthur TRAYLOR and Eliza Blankenship, dau. of James Blankenship who consents. Sur. John Rowlett, Jr. Wit. Peter Moody. Married 14 February by Rev. Joseph Gill. p. 107.

21 November 1809. Bawall TRAYLOR and Sarah Goode. Married by Rev. Charles Forsee, Skinquarter Baptist Church. Ministers'. Returns p. 402.

12 January 1789. Buckner TRAYLOR and Mary Handy. Married by Rev. John Cameron, Rector of Bristol Parish, Episcopal Church.

10 February 1806. Edward TRAYLOR and Mary Traylor. Sur. William.N. Traylor. Married 13 February by Rev. Thomas Lafon, Church of Christ. p. 81.

3 March 1775. Frederick TRAYLOR and Ann Edwards. Marke Edwards consents for Ann; no relationship stated. Sur. John Edwards. Wit. Humphries Traylor. p. 4.

20 February 1806. George TRAYLOR and Nancy Gates. Married by Rev. Charles Forsee, Skinquarter Baptist Church. Ministers' Returns p. 400.

30 October 1813. Herbert TRAYLOR and Catharine Stratton Stringer, 21 years of age 18 Mar. 1813. Sur. James Perdue. Wit. Page Vaden. p. 122.

8 February 1813. Isham TRAYLOR and Elizabeth C. Lockett, dau. of Elam Lockett who consents. Sur. Robert Lockett. p. 119.

21 November 1814. John TRAYLOR and Catharine Burton, 21 years of age, dau. of John Burton. Sur. Peter Moody. Married 23 November by Rev. Joseph Gill, Jr. p. 126.

19 June 1805. Joe TRAYLOR and Elizabeth Moore, dau. of William Moore. Sur. Robert Andrews. Wit. Parke Poindexter and William S. Dance. p. 77.

13 September 1805. Littleberry TRAYLOR and Nancy Andrews, 21 years of age, dau. of Elizabeth Andrews who consents. Sur. Parke Poindexter. Wit. William S. Dance. Married by Rev. Eleazar Clay, Baptist. p. 78.

_____ 1788. Micajah TRAYLOR and Jenney Chasteen. Married by Rev. John Goode. Ministers' Returns p. 373.

24 August 1799. Thomas TRAYLOR and Mary Stiles, dau. of Sarah Stiles who consents. Wit. Liza Stiles and William Stiles. Married by Rev. Thomas Hardie, Methodist. p. 497.

5 July 1815. Thomas TRAYLOR and Elizabeth F. Watkins. Sur. Archibald Hatcher. Married 8 July by Rev. Thomas Lafon, Church of Christ. p. 130.

14 October 1780. William TRAYLOR and Sally Hancock. Sur. George Hancock. p. 12.

5 May 1799. William N. TRAYLOR and Elizabeth Winfree. Consent of Samuel Clarke for Elizabeth; no relationship stated. Sur. Richard Taylor. Married by Rev. Eleazer Clay, Baptist. p. 55.

_____ 1803. William TRAYLOR and Sandel Traylor. Married by Rev. Eleazar Clay, Baptist. Ministers' Returns p. 397.

7 June 1813. William TRAYLOR and Mary Ann Cross, dau. of William Cross who consents. Sur. Andrew Cross. Married 11 June by Rev. Thomas Lafon, Church of Christ. p. 120.

10 December 1782. Alexander TRENT and Ann Anderson. Francis Goode consents for Ann; no relationship stated. This is consent only. p. 17.

6 February 1779. John TRENT and Sarah Welch. Sur. John Welch. p. 8.

3 October 1783. Thomas TRENT and Elizabeth Edwards. Wit. Mary Edwards and Peterfield Trent. This is consent only. p. 19.

23 November 1805. David TROKES and Martha Clarke, dau. of William Clarke who consents. Sur. David Patterson, Jr. p. 79.

12 December 1814. John TRUEMAN and Nancy Hobbs, 21 years of age. Sur. Randolph Martin. Married 13 December by Rev. Henry Bridgewater. p. 127.

6 January 1811. Anderson TUCKER and Nancy Abrams, 21 years of age. Sur. John Cordle. Anderson Tucker of Dinwiddie County. p. 106.

24 November 1784. Branch TUCKER and Millicent Cheatham. Married by Rev. John Goode. Ministers' Returns p. 369.

19 September 1778. St. George TUCKER and Frances Randolph, widow of John Randolph. Sur. Jerman Baker. Wit. Fanny Banister and Ann Ward. She was born 24 Sept. 1752, dau. of Theodick and Frances (Bolling) Bland. m. 1st 9 Mar. 1769 John Randolph. She d. 18 Jan. 1788. St. George Tucker b. 29 June 1752; d. 1827. p. 7.

17 May 1803. John TUCKER and Agness Epps Goode. Wit. Thomas Goode and Martha Hamlin. This is consent only. p. 67.

15 September 1808. William N. TUCKER and Laurana Perdue, dau. of John Perdue who consents and is surety. Married by Rev. Eleazar Clay, Baptist. p. 92.

_____ 1802. Joseph TUNBULL and Martha Boles. Married by Rev. Charles Forsee, Minister of Skinquarter Baptist Church. Ministers' Returns p. 395.

26 January 1802. Edmund TUNSTALL and Elizabeth Smith. Sur. John Magee. Wit. John H. Smith and Eliza M. Smith. Edmund Tunstall of Pittsylvania County. p. 64.

10 October 1791. William TUNSTILL and Sally Britton, dau. of William Britton who consents. Married 15 October by Rev. Needler Robinson, Rector of Dale Parish, Episcopal Church. p. 33.

7 December 1800. John TURNER and Nancy Brown. Wit. John Johnson. This is consent only. Married 25 December by Rev. Benjamin Watkins. p. 61.

4 October 1805. Pleasant A. TURNER and Martha Lapraid (Laprade), dau. of John Lapraid (Laprade) who consents and is surety. Married 5 October by Rev. Thomas Lafon, Church of Christ. p. 78.

3 December 1808. Samuel TURNER and Mary Clarke, dau. of William Clarke who consents. Sur. Matthew Brown. Wit. David Trokes. p. 94.

_____ 1792. Henry TURPIN and Elizabeth Roberson. Married by Rev. Eleazer Clay, Baptist. Ministers' Returns p. 380.

9 October 1773. Hezekiah TURPIN and Jane Cheatham. Sur. James Cheatham. p. 3.

1794-1795. Jeremiah TURPIN and Anne Robertson. Married by Rev. Eleazer Clay, Baptist. Ministers' Returns p. 382.

8 September 1779. Thomas TURPIN and Rachel Cheetwood. Sur. John Cheetwood. p. 10.

15 March 1808. William Archer TURPIN and Rebecca Smith. Humphrey Sale, guardian of Rebecca, consents for her. Sur. Peter F. Smith. Wit. John H. Smith. p. 90.

24 July 1804. Micajah TYRE and Sarah Auter, dau. of Sarah Auter who consents. Sur. Jere Ligon. Could this be Tyree? p. 72.

1 March 1808. Marshall VADEN and Apellona Vaden. Married by Rev. John Cox, Methodist. Ministers' Returns p. 401.

11 April 1804. William VADEN and Stacy Blankenship, dau. of Beaviley (Beverley?) Blankenship who consents. Sur. Beavily Standley. Could this be Beverly Stanard? p. 71.

24 December 1796. Wilson VADEN and Dysey Moore. Sur. Ellick Moore. Wit. Thomas Finney. Married by Rev. Eleazer Clay, Baptist. Page 485 says Dicey. p. 46.

12 August 1785. John VADEN and Hanna Nunnally, of age. This is consent only. Married by Rev. Eleazer Clay, Baptist, who says Hannah. p. 23.

17 January 1789. John VARNIER and Mary Marshall. Married by Rev. Richard Garrettson of the town of Petersburg. Ministers' Returns p. 376.

10 March 1812. John VARNIER, Jr. and Nancy Clayton, dau. of John Clayton who consents. Sur. Thomas Clayton. p. 113.

18 March 1812. John VARNIER, Sr. and Sarah P. Bass. Sur. Thomas Watkins. Wit. J. R. Bradley. p. 113.

11 December 1802. Peter VARNIER and Frances Moore. Married by Rev. Needler Robinson, Rector of Dale Parish, Episcopal Church. Ministers' Returns p. 391.

25 August 1807. Thomas VARNIER and Nancy Franklin, widow of John Franklin. Sur. William Varnier. Married 26 August by Rev. Henry Featherstone, Sr. who says Varner. p. 87.

12 December 1783. Abraham VAUGHAN and Michal Folks. Married by Rev. William Hickman, Minister of Skinquarter Baptist Church. Ministers' Returns p. 369.

9 November 1785. Gabriel VEST and Tabitha _____. Married by Rev. John Goode. Ministers' Returns p. 371.

9 April 1798. Henry VEST and Fanney Perdue. Married by Rev. Nathan Anderson, Methodist. Ministers' Returns p. 388.

10 December 1810. Henry VEST and Elizabeth Baugh, 21 years of age, dau. of James Baugh, deceased. Sur. Philip H. Vest. p. 105.

23 December 1807. Hezekiah VEST and Johanna Dumas, widow of Benjamin Dumas. Sur. William Smith. p. 88.

8 May 1815. Obadiah H. VEST and Senath Smith. Sur. Archibald Franklin. Married 13 May by Rev. Joseph Gill, Jr. See Obadiah H. West. p. 130.

1797-1799. Phillip VEST and Polley Baugh. Married by Rev. Eleazer Clay, Baptist. Minsiters' Returns p. 392.

15 May 1810. John VICKERS and Marinda Alvis, dau. of Forest Alvis, deceased. Sur. Robert Goode. p. 102.

11 November 1793. Obadiah WADE and Caroline Walthall, dau. of Elizabeth Walthall who consents. Wit. Henry Walthall. Obadiah Wade of Goochland County. This is consent only. Omitted from p. 37. p. 57.

21 December 1799. John WAGGENER and Ann Morgan, 21 years of age, dau. of John Morgan who consents. Wit. John Kleinhoff and Sarah Kleinhoff. This is consent only. Married by Rev. Eleazer Clay, Baptist. p. 57.

23 December 1800. John WAGGONER and Ann Morgan. Sur. Isaac Skelton. Wit. John Cary. p. 61.

13 November 1804. Edward WALFORD and Susanna A. Goodwin. This is consent only. p. 74.

20 December 1806. Edward WALFORD and Ann Cobb, dau. of
Elizabeth Cobb who consents. Sur. Joseph C. Brown. Wit. Phili
Michael. p. 84.

12 August 1811. John R. WALK and Martha B. Branch. Sur. Thoma
Branch. p. 109.

14 December 1793. George WALKER and Judith Finny Branch, dau.
of Lucy Branch who consents. Wit. Edward Branch and D. Coleman
This is consent only. p. 37.

29 April 1813. Lancelot WALKER and Salley Green, 21 years of
age, dau. of William Green. Sur. James Walden. Married by Rev
Thomas Lafon, Church of Christ. p. 120.

5 January 1813. Thomas WALLER and Sarah Sasseen, 21 years of
age. Sur. Walter Scott Winfree. p. 118.

_____ _____ 1801. Francis WALTHALL and Phebe Elam. Married by
Rev. Charles Forsee, Minister of Skinquarter Baptist Church.
Ministers' Returns p. 395.

11 May 1813. Francis WALTHALL and Rebecca Andrews, 21 years of
age. Sur. Charles E. Featherstone. Married 12 May by Rev.
Thomas Lafon, Church of Christ. p. 120.

27 April 1793. Henry WALTHALL and Nancy Walthall. Archibald
Walthall, guardian of Nancy, consents for her. Married by Rev.
Thomas Hardie, Methodist. p. 497.

28 March 1801. Henry WALTHALL and Elizabeth Batts. Married by
Rev. Thomas Hardie, Methodist. Ministers' Returns p. 395.

9 September 1815. John WALTHALL and Harriet Frances Stratton,
dau. of John Stratton. Sur. Walthall Hatcher. Married 14
September by Rev. B. H. Rice of Petersburg. p. 131.

12 February 1796. Marley WALTHALL and Peggy Jones Batte, dau.
of Thomas Batte who consents. Sur. Henry Walthall and Chamblin
Batte. Married 20 February by Rev. Needler Robinson, Rector of
Dale Parish, Episcopal Church. p. 43.

15 November 1809. Marley WALTHALL and Miranda Jackson, dau. of
Peter Jackson, deceased. Sur. Henry Walthall. p. 99.

2 April 1773. Richard WALTHALL and Catherine Walthall. Sur.
Gerrard Walthall. Wit. Benjamin Watkins. p. 2.

17 December 1795. Richard WALTHALL and Judith Flournoy.
Married by Rev. James Rucks. Ministers' Returns p. 383.

3 July 1802. Richard WALTHALL and Elizabeth Walthall. Married
by Rev. Charles Forsee, Minister of Skinquarter Baptist Church.
Ministers' Returns p. 393.

9 January 1804. Richard WALTHALL and Sally Hix, dau. of William
Hix who consents and is surety. p. 70.

3 November 1773. William WALTHALL and Sophia Farley. Sur.
Archibald Walthall. p. 3.

29 October 1782. William WALTHALL and Martha Wooldridge. Sur.
Richard Elam. p. 16.

_____ 1800. William WALTHALL and Salley Chalkley. Married
by Rev. Eleazar Clay, Baptist. Ministers' Returns p. 393.

_____ 1791. William WARE and Anne Robertson. Married by
Rev. Walthall Robertson, Baptist. Return dated 14 November
1791. Ministers' Returns p. 377.

8 February 1791. John WARREN and Sarah Puckett. Married by Rev.
Needler Robinson, Rector of Dale Parish, Episcopal Church.
Ministers' Returns p. 375.

12 October 1807. Robert WARREN and Caty B. Vivion. Sur. James
Clark, Jr. p. 87.

13 March 1812. Clements WATKINS and Martha Cunningham, 21 years
of age. Sur. Richard Jones. p. 113.

26 April 1800. John WATKINS and Peggy Short. Married by Rev.
Benjamin Watkins. Ministers' Returns p. 390.

25 May 1803. John WATKINS and Ann Banks. Thomas C. Martin,
guardian of Ann, consents for her. Sur. William Winfree. Wit.
William Banks. Married 26 May by Rev. Benjamin Watkins. p. 67.

13 January 1812. John WATKINS and Anna P. Boisseau. Sur.
Daniel Boisseau. p. 112.

22 July 1785. Joseph WATKINS and Judith Winfrey. Married by
Rev. William Leigh, Rector of Manchester Parish. Episcopal Church.
Ministers' Retuens p. 369.

5 January 1804. Matthew WATSON and Elizabeth Graves, dau. of
Arthur Graves who consents. Wit. Matthew Graves. This is
consent only. p. 70.

30 April 1807. Benjamin WATKINSON and Mary Condry. Married by
Rev. Charles Forsee, Skinquarter Baptist Church. Ministers'
Returns p. 400.

17 June 1784. Philip WATT and Mary Wray. Sur. John Foulkes.
See Philip Ott. p. 21.

5 October 1796. Thomas WATTON and Elizabeth Pankey, dau. of
Mary Pankey who consents. Sur. Benjamin Elliott. Wit. Judith
Pankey. p. 45.

22 December 1803. William WATTS and Mary B. Smith, dau. of
Obadiah Smith who consents. Wit. Chism. Austin and John Brooks.
p. 70.

20 December 1791. Andrew WAUGH and Nancy Archer, dau. of Ann
Archer who consents. Sur. Instance Hall. Wit. William Hall.
Married 22 December by Rev. Robert Walthall, Methodist. p. 33.

21 November 1801. William WEAKS and Pheby Mann. Married by Rev
Thomas Hardie, Methodist. Ministers' Returns p. 395.

1 February 1812. John WEBSTER and Martha Gibbs, dau. of Thomas
Gibbs who consents and is surety. p. 112.

15 February 1808. Richard K. WEISEGER and Martha Goode, dau. of
William Goode who consents. Sur. Robert Goode. p. 89.

31 March 1808. Washington WEISEGER and Polly C. Talley, dau. of
James Talley who consents. Sur. William D. Talley. p. 90.

3 September 1798. Daniel WEISIGER and Sarah Branch, dau. of
Thomas Branch who consents. Wit. Benjamin Branch and Thomas
Branch. This is consent only. p. 52.

13 February 1815. Daniel WEISIGER and Seigniora T. Smith. Sur.
R. D. Murchie. Wit. William Bradshaw. p. 128.

3 January 1806. David WEISIGER, Jr. and Nancy Branch, dau. of
Thomas Branch who consents and is surety. p. 81.

22 December 1810. Baker WELLS and Elizabeth P. Rowlett, 21 years
of age, dau. of John Rowlett, deceased. Sur. Hobson Chalkley.
p. 106.

19 December 1805. Dickerson WELLS and Phebe Rowlett, dau. of
William Rowlett, Jr. who consents. Sur. John Rowlett. p. 80.

26 August 1814. Giles WELLS and Rebecca Gibbs, dau. of John
Gibbs who consents. Sur. Alexander Gibbs. Wit. John P. Crump.
Married 1 September by Rev. Joseph Gill, Jr. p. 126.

4 May 1798. Isham WELLS and Elizabeth Winfree. Sur. John
Wilkinson. Wit. John Markham, Jr. Married 7 June by Rev. Thomas
Hardie, Methodist. p. 51.

29 December 1785. Littleberry WELLS and Polly Goode. Married
by Rev. William Leigh, Rector of Manchester Parish, Episcopal
Church. Ministers' Returns p. 370.

13 November 1803. Michael WELLS, Jr. and Frances Rowlett, dau.
of John Rowlett who consents. Wit. John Y. Covington and Barker
Wells. Married by Rev. Thomas Hardie, Methodist. p. 69.

12 January 1796. William WELLS and Martha Frankling. Married
by Rev. Thomas Hardie, Methodist. Ministers' Returns p. 383.

29 March 1806. William C. WELLS and Sophia Clarke. Sur. Stephen
G. Wells. p. 81.

17 March 1797. James WEST and Sally Womack. Married by Rev.
Needler Robinson, Rector of Dale Parish, Episcopal Church.
Ministers' Returns p. 385.

13 May 1815. Obadiah H. WEST and Senath Smith. Married by Rev.
Joseph Gill, Jr. (I think West is right). See Obadiah H. Vest.
Ministers' Returns p. 409.

28 March 1814. Hartwell WESTMORELAND and Mary D. Branch, 21
years of age, dau. of Edward Branch. Sur. Archibald Hatcher.
Hartwell Westmoreland of Dinwiddie County. Married 9 April by
Rev. Thomas Lafon, Church of Christ. p. 124.

17 February 1809. Jesse WHITE and Patsey Hancock, dau. of
Ananias Hancock who consents. Sur. John Hancock. Wit. Robert
Allen. p. 96.

28 December 1808. Joshua WHITE and Patience Cole, dau. of
William Cole who consents and is surety. p. 94.

22 December 1815. Joseph WHITFORD and Rebecca Puckett, 21 years of age. Sur. John Walthall. Married 23 Dec. by Rev. B. H. Rice of Petersburg. p. 132.

1 October 1804. Matthew S. WHITLOCK and Priscilla Pride. Sur. John A. Pride. Married by Rev. Needler Robinson, Rector of Dale Parish, Episcopal Church. p. 73.

21 June 1815. John WHITMORE and Nancy Elam, dau. of John Elam, deceased, and Elizabeth Brackett. Sur. Wiley Whitmore. Married 7 July by Rev. Thomas Lafon, Church of Christ. p. 130.

4 June 1778. Herbert WHITTON and Mary Folks. Sur. John Face. p. 6.

19 February 1791. Thomas WHITWORTH and Jeane Branch. Wit. Walter Ford and Samuel Ford. This is consent only. p. 32.

6 June 1810. Thomas WHITWORTH and Anne Baugh. Sur. Allen Whitworth. Wit. John Baugh and Arthur Baugh. p. 102.

18 September 1812. Daniel WILKINSON and Sarah Lester, dau. of Jere Lester who consents. Sur. Jeremiah Clarke. p. 116.

4 March 1780. John WILKINSON and Elizabeth Moody. Sur. Joseph Cole. p. 11.

19 May 1789. John WILKINSON and Maggy Wells. Married by Rev. Needler Robinson, Rector of Dale Parish, Episcopal Church. Ministers' Returns p. 374.

3 March 1809. John WILKINSON and Saley Pirdee. Married by Rev. Charles Forsee, Skinquarter Baptist Church. Ministers' Returns p. 402.

17 March 1810. Joseph WILKINSON and Betsy Robertson, dau. of Jonas Robertson who consents and is surety. p. 100.

27 August 1779. Mack WILKINSON and Mary Jackson. Sur. Joseph Wilkinson. p. 10.

24 November 1796. Robert WILKINSON and Wilmouth Wineford. Married by Rev. James Rucks. Ministers' Returns p. 384.

22 June 1813. Robert WILKINSON and Polly Bass, dau. of Thomas Bass who consents and is surety. p. 120.

2 May 1815. Robert J. WILKINSON and Sally Wooldridge. Sur. John Cole. Wit. John P. Crump. p. 130.

11 December 1794. Hatton WILLIAMS and Elizabeth Dillion.
Married by Rev. Needler Robinson, Rector of Dale Parish, Episcopal Church. Ministers' Returns p. 378.

12 November 1792. John WILLIAMS and Clara Phillips. Married by
Rev. Needler Robinson, Rector of Dale Parish, Episcopal Church.
Ministers' Returns p. 377.

12 June 1797. John WILLIAMS and Mary Bottom, dau. of Thomas
Bottom who consents. Wit. William Moss and Francis Bottom.
This is consent only. Married by Rev. Eleazer Clay, Baptist.
p. 47.

25 December 1797. Joseph WILLIAMS and Nancy Hallam Smith. Wit.
James Smith and John Smith. This is consent only. Married by
Rev. Thomas Hardie, Methodist. p. 497.

11 March 1804. Powell WILLIAMS and Polly Farmer. Married by
Rev. James Rucks. Ministers' Returns p. 398.

16 June 1782. Robert WILLIAMSON and Martha Smith. Sur. Philip
Smith. p. 16.

1 December 1798. Robert WILLIAMSON and Phebe Baugh. Sur.
William Fuqua. Married 15 December by Rev. Thomas Hardie,
Methodist. p. 53.

_____ 1803. William WILLIS and Miney Winfrey. Married by
Rev. Eleazar Clay, Baptist. Ministers' Returns p. 397.

_____ 1790. Thomas WILLS and Lucy Wilkinson. Married by
Rev. Eleazer Clay, Baptist. Ministers' Returns p. 376.

14 January 1805. Daniel WILLSON and Betsey Blankenship, 21 years
of age, dau. of Stephen Blankenship. Sur. Robert McLelland.
Married 19 January by Rev. Charles Hopkins. p. 75.

14 February 1812. Ephraim WILLSON and Elizabeth Roberts. Sur.
Littleton Willson. p. 112.

15 November 1815. George WILLSON and Mazey Andrews, 21 years of
age,. Sur. Peter Gill. Married 18 November by Rev. Joseph Gill,
Jr. p. 131.

6 April 1805. Lodowick WILLSON and Dorotha Dunnivant, 21 years
of age, dau. of Nancy Dunnivant. Sur. Ramsey Dunnivant. Wit.
William Wyatt. p. 76.

11 January 1808. Lodowick WILLSON and Betsey Jackson Moore, dau.
of Mark Moore who consents. Sur. Alexander Moore. Wit. William
S. Dance. p. 89.

25 August 1810. Samuel WILLSON and Lockey Andrews. Sur. Thoma
Franklin. Married by Rev. Thomas Lafon, Church of Christ. p.
104.

2 December 1774. Tom Branch WILLSON and Judith Friend. Sur.
George Markham. p. 4.

12 April 1798. Henry WILSON and Martha Mann. Married by Rev.
Thomas Hardie, Methodist. Ministers' Returns p. 388.

11 July 1803. Thomas WILSON and Amey Franklin. Sur. William
Dodson. p. 67.

11 August 1789. Archer WINFREE and Phebe Blankenship. Sur.
Claiborne Puckett. Married by Rev. Needler Robinson, Rector of
Dale Parish, Episcopal Church. p. 28.

1 March 1798. Archer WINFREE and Sandall Blankenship. Sur.
Beverly Stanard. Wit. Thomas Finney. Married by Rev. Eleazer
Clay, Baptist. p. 50.

23 December 1806. Francis WINFREE and Sally Burton, dau. of
Thomas Burton. Sur. Stephen Branch. p. 84.

5 January 1807. Henry WINFREE, Jr. and Elizabeth Winfree, dau.
of Major Winfree who consents. Sur. Valentine Winfree, Jr.
Wit. Major Cheatham. p. 85.

10 April 1809. James W. WINFREE and Lucy Patterson, dau. of
Daniel Patterson. Sur. Valentine Winfree, Jr. p. 96.

14 November 1808. John WINFREE and Sarah Hill, dau. of Sarah
Hill who consents. Sur. Valentine Winfree, Jr. Wit. Sarah Hill
and John Hill. p. 93.

28 March 1805. Matthew WINFREE and Ann Flournoy. Married by
Rev. Benjamin Watkins. Ministers' Returns p. 399.

11 January 1808. Nelson WINFREE and Frances Willson Vaden, dau
of George Vaden, deceased. Sur. John Wilkinson. Wit. John
Wilson. p. 89.

14 February 1814. Peter WINFREE and Phebe Patram, dau. of
Francis Patram who consents and is surety. Married 23 February
by Rev. Joseph Gill, Jr. p. 124.

5 June 1812. Valentine WINFREE and Mary Green Mann, dau. of
John Mann who consents and is surety. p. 114.

21 July 1807. William WINFREE and Lucy Bass, dau. of Archibald Bass who consents. Sur. Robert B. Cabell. Both are mentioned in Archibald Bass' settlement of estate 11 Feb. 1822. p. 86.

2 January 1784. Henry WINFREY and Elizabeth Jarratt. Sur. Archelus Jarratt. p. 20.

13 December 1779. Reubin WINFREY and Mary Cobb. Sur. Thomas Bridgewater. p. 10.

8 December 1794. John WOMACK and Ann Baugh. Married by Rev. Needler Robinson, Rector of Dale Parish. Episcopal Church. Ministers' Returns p. 378.

9 May 1791. William WOMACK and Elizabeth Purkinson, dau. of Robert Purkinson who consents. Wit. Ezekiel Jackson. This is consent only. Married 9 June by Rev. John Cameron, Rector of Bristol Parish, Episcopal Church, who says Perkinson. p. 32.

2 February 1804. William WOMACK and Polly Davis. Married by Rev. Henry Featherstone, Sr. Ministers' Returns p. 398.

23 January 1779. Guliemus WOOD and Mary Adkins. Sur. Robert Adkins. p. 8.

15 October 1801. Capt. John WOODARD and Sarah Clark, dau. of Sarah Clark who consents. This is consent only. p. 64.

_____ _____ 1800. Joseph WOOD and Polley Brooks. Married by Rev. Eleazar Clay, Baptist. Ministers' Returns p. 393.

7 July 1812. Robert WOOD and Sally Gregory, dau. of Thomas Gregory who consents. Sur. Thomas Gregory, Jr. p. 114.

5 September 1783. George WOODSON and _____ _____. Sur. George Markham. Omitted from p. 19. p. 57.

30 October 1794. Tarlton WOODSON and Ann Friend, over 21 years of age, dau. of Sarah Friend. Sur. Thomas Friend. Married 13 November by Rev. Needler Robinson, Rector of Dale Parish, Episcopal Church. p. 39.

8 September 1795. Archibald WOOLDRIDGE and Sally Ellyson, dau. of Milly Ellyson who consents. Thomas Wooldridge, father of Archibald, consents for him. Sur. John Roberts. Wit. William Finney, Edward Wooldridge, John Roberts, Jr., and William Sowell. p. 42.

14 November 1809. Chesley WOOLDRIDGE and Elizabeth Johnson.
Sur. Samuel Woody. p. 98.

15 November 1782. Daniel WOOLDRIDGE and Ann Grant Spencer. Joh
Bott, guardian of Ann, consents for her. Sur. Nicholas Robertso
p. 17.

9 May 1814. Daniel WOOLDRIDGE and Sarah Hill, widow of Robert
Hill. Sur. Parke Poindexter. Married 24 May by Rev. Thomas
Anserson, Sr. p. 125.

1 November 1777. Edward WOOLDRIDGE and Mary Simpson, dau. of
Andrew Simpson. Sur. Edward Farley. Wit. Stephen Childress.
p. 5.

18 February 1785. Josiah WOOLDRIDGE and Martha Trabue. Wit.
Edward Trabue and Stephen Trabue. (her brothers). Martha was
dau. of John James Trabue and Olymphia Dupuy. p. 22.

7 May 1793. Seth WOOLDRIDGE and Peggy Elam, dau. of Daniel
Elam, Sr. who consents. Sur. William Elam, Jr. Wit. Samuel
Harris. p. 36.

5 October 1772. Thomas WOOLDRIDGE and Mary Ceaye (relict)
(widow). Sur. George Markham. p. 1.

14 September 1800. William WOOLDRIDGE and Mary Trent, dau. of
John Trent who consents. Wit. Anderson Johnson and Mary
Johnson. This is consent only. Married 16 September by Rev.
Benjamin Watkins. p. 61.

_____ 1793. David WORSHAM and Jemima Dunavant. Married
by Rev. Eleazer Clay, Baptist. Ministers' Returns p. 381.

19 November 1778. Henry WORSHAM and Agnes Kelly. Sur. John
Kelly. p. 7.

21 December 1799. Jeremiah WORSHAM and Mary Ann Cashon, dau. of
Burwell Cashon who consents. Sur. James Cashon. (I think this
name is Cashion.) Married by Rev. Eleazer Clay, Baptist. p. 57

_____ 1803. John WORSHAM and Mary Wash. Married by Rev.
Eleazar Clay, Baptist. Ministers' Returns p. 397.

June 1787-June 1788. Peter WORSHAM and Michal Wilinson.
Married by Rev. Eleazer Clay, Baptist. Ministers' Returns p.
372.

13 January 1778. Thomas WORSHAM and Martha Moseley. Sur. Richard Wilkinson. p. 6.

15 July 1786. William WORSHAM and Clarissa Walthall. Married by Rev. William Leigh, Rector of Manchester Parish, Episcopal Church. Ministers' Returns p. 370.

8 September 1809. William WORSHAM and Elizabeth Addison, widow of John Addison. Sur. Henry Walthall. p. 98.

___ March 1803. John WOTTON and Sally Dillion. Married by Rev. Henry Featherstone, Sr. Ministers' Returns p. 396.

10 February 1812. Randolph WYATT and Tabitha Belcher, dau. of Isham Belcher who consents and is surety. Wit. Francis Belcher and Robert Belcher. Married 13 February by Rev. Joseph Gill. p. 112.

6 February 1804. Thomas WYATT and Nancy Caulfield, dau. of William Caulfield who consents. Sur. Archer Winfree. Wit. Elizabeth Caulfield. p. 70.

19 August 1806. William WYATT and Elizabeth Dunnavant, dau. of William Dunnavant who consents and is surety. p. 82.

___ October 1803. John YARRINGTON and Elizabeth Eggleston. W. Claiborne, guardian of Elizabeth, consents for her. This is consent only. p. 69.

26 September 1811. John ZIMMERMAN and Elizabeth Blankenship, 21 years of age. Sur. Daniel Blankenship. Married 28 September by Rev. Joseph Gill. p. 110.

Brander, Eliza 20
Breade, Elizabeth 61
Brechan, Elizabeth 3; Polley 20
Bridgewater, Mary 7,79
Brintle, Drusilla 91; Polley 62;
   Susanna 52
Britton, Elizabeth 42,49,101;
   Nancy 10; Polly 43,101; Rebec-
   ca 64; Sally 121
Broadie - Broodie, Margaret 84;
   Mary 13
Brooks, Elizabeth 21; Lucy 29,
   103; Mary 47; Polley 131;
   Rebecca 111; Sarah 108
Brown, Locky 104; Martha 57;
   Mary 57; Nancy 48,121; Obe-
   dience 66
Bruce, Eliza 30; Martha 61
Brummall, Edith 73; Hany 8; Mary
   101; Obedience 26; Rhoda 69;
   Wealthy Ann 49
Bryant, Jane 83; Maria M. 103
Bryan, Mary 62
Bryars - Bryers, Lucy 24; Polley
   64
Buck, Mariah A. 6
Burfoot, Ann 35; Martha 32
Burke, Lucy 84
Burton, Anne 64; Catharine 120;
   Dolly 62; Elizabeth 73; Martha
   73; Mary 93,99; Polly 74,93;
   Saba 38; Sally 25,130; Sally
   Phillips 85
Butler, Rebecca 26; Sally 26
Byrd, Milly 62

Cabell, Eliza 89
Cacy - Cacey - Cayce, Annuse 77;
   Anusze 78; Mary 111; Priscilla
   78
Calvin, Alice 47
Carter, Eliza 61; Elizabeth 55;
   Polly 64
Cary, Ann 103; Elizabeth 36,75;
   Judith 24; Mary 92
Cashon, Mary Ann 132; Phebe 99
Caulfield, Nancy 133
Ceaye, Mary 132
Chalkley, Ann 110; Judith 67;
   Levinia 102; Patsey 48; Ridley
   33; Sally 125; Sarah 64; Tabi-
   tha 2
Chamberlain, Nancy 71
Chappell, Jemima 72; Nanch(?) 89;
   Oney 52; Polly 58; Sarah 96;
   Susanna 60
Charleton, Polly 14; Reaney 14
Chasteen, Jenny 120
Chatham, Margaret 90
Cheatham, Angelica 90; Angelica
   Epps 40; Ann 59,76,105; Dinah
   81; Elizabeth 47(2),92; Eliza-
   beth Green 50; Jane 122; Lemiry
   70; Lurina 18; Margaret 28;
   Martha 11,59,67; Mary 2,63,
   88; Mary Ann Pride 92; Michel
   44; Millicent 121; Patience 9;
   Patty 11,22; Phebe 9,44,78;
   Polly 20(2),56; Prudence 52;
   Rebecca 28,90; Sally 30; Sarah
   25; Tabitha 20,33,60,90

Cheetwood, Rachel 122
Chockley, Lucy 74
Christian, Lucy 33
Claiborne, Mary Leigh 31; Violet
Clark - Clarke, Elizabeth 61;
   Bidy 57; Jane 69; Margaret 11;
   Martha 54,121; Mary 122; Nancy
   87; Patsey 106; Phebe 115; Rhod
   33; Sarah 131; Sinai 105; Sophi
   127; Tabitha 7
Clay, Anna 106; Dorcas 61; Eliza-
   beth 91; Jane 118; Lavinia 2;
   Martha S. 24
Clayton, Fanny 110; Lucy 54; Nanc
   122; Sarah 110
Cleatin, Disey 59
Cliborne, Margaret 85
Coates, Elizabeth 31(2)
Cobb - Cobbs, Ann 124; Elizabeth
   7,86; Hannah 83; Mary 94,100,
   131; Mary B. 85(2); Sally M. 73
Cochrane, Catherine Anna 80
Cogbill, Frances 7; Phebe 8,42;
   Polly Bass 34; Rebecca 110;
   Sally 59,66; Susanna S. 37;
   Susanna Stith 26,75
Cole, Barbara 93; Patience 127;
   Polly 114
Conbusia, Hororiah 81
Condry, Elizabeth 106; Mary 126
Conner, Nelly 116
Cook, Hannah 73
Cousins, Anne 24; Elizabeth 38,
   52; Martha 1; Nancy 117; Sarah
   67
Covington, Elizabeth 34; Martha
   98,104; Mary 46,101(2)
Cox, Catharine 98; Damaris 101;
   Elizabeth 40,63; Frances 103;
   Maryan 23; Polley 73; Rhoda 26;
   Sally 44,62; Sarah 78; Susanna
   112; Tabitha Randolph 80
Cozby - Cosby, Martha 36
Crawley, Frances 114
Cross, Catharine 70; Lucy 70;
   Mary Ann 120
Crostick, Amey 11
Crump, Peggy 49; Susannah 108
Cunliff, Eliza Ann 66
Cunningham, Agness 18; Elizabeth
   101; Martha 125; Nancy 40;
   Sarah 6
Cuthell, Martha 101

Dance, Agness 118; Elizabeth 13(2
   Lucy H. 87; Martha 77,93; Mary
   99,104; Nancy 24; Patsey 13;
   Polly 4,95; Rhode 72
Daniel, Amy 66
Danlavey, Elizabeth 74
Davis, Betty 56; Elizabeth 74,99;
   Nancy 56; Polly 119,131; Sarah
Deaton, Polly 19
Dillion, Elizabeth 129; Sally 133
Dockett, Anne 11
Dodd, Margaret 42; Polly 60
Dodson, Ann 50,67; Mariah 89;
   Mary 89
Donald, Ann 116
Downman, Elizabeth Osborne 69;
   Fanny 97

Dudley, Martha 43
Dumas, Johanna 123
Duncan, Charlotte Smith 54; Nancy
  Gilliam 40
Dunlavy, Jane 113; Mary 71
Dunnavant - Dunnivant, Caroline
  78; Dorotha 129; Elizabeth
  133; Jane 87; Jean 78; Jemima
  132; Jinsey 78; Susannah 82
Dyer, Nancy 4; Pheby 5
Dyson, Betsy 22; Jane 56; Mary
  57; Sally 110

Eanes, Ann-Anne 40,57; Edy 96;
  Frances Rowlett 58; Martha 21;
  Nancy 52; Polly 21; Susannah
  G. 36
Edwards, Ann 119; Elizabeth 120;
  Mary 2, Mary Ann 70; Nancy 98;
  Rebecca 108; Susannah 80
Eggleston, Elizabeth 133
El---, Nancy 9
Elam, Ann 10; Betsy Ann 43;
  Dinah 43; Elizabeth 18,25,29,
  33,66; Joanna 16; Martha 44,
  103; Mary 8; Nancy 128; Peggy
  132; Phebe 29,44,77,124; Phebe
  Baugh 59; Phebe Branch 59;
  Polly 93,98,111; Prudence 10;
  Sally 60; Sarah 25; Susanna 45
Ellett - Elliott, Anne 7; Eliza-
  beth 88; Martha 30; Sarah 37;
  Wealthy Ann 23
Ellis, Pheby 30; Rebecca 34;
  Salley 27
Ellison - Ellyson, Frances 29;
  Mene 73; Nancy 92; Pity 9;
  Polly 74; Sally 131
Eppes, Ann 19; Polly 117
Evans, Priscilla 8

Farlager, Mary 111
Farley, Sophia 125
Farmer, Anne 37(2); Caty 50;
  Cynthia 113; Dicey 27; Dolley
  55; Dorothy 47; Elizabeth 9,
  13,104,113; Jane 113; Judith
  89; Judith Moore 47; Mary 54;
  Nancy 35,76; Page 71; Phebe
  21,26,27,43,50; Polly 63,129;
  Rhoda 16,17; Sarah 113; Sophia
  23; Tabitha 16,18
Fargus, Phebe 83
Fargusson-Fergusson-Furgusson,
  Appy 106; Elizabeth 12,18,34;
  Jinsey 10; Mary 69; Masey 19;
  Michel Matilda 91; Miny 111;
  Nancy 48; Polly 62,65; Rhoda
  89; Sally 12; Sarah 90
Featherstone, Elizabeth 34; Mary
  Ann 33; Phebe 71; Sarah 63
Finney, Elizabeth 41
Fleming, Jane W. 112; Mary
  Bolling 112
Flournoy, Ann 130; Edith 17;
  Elizabeth 43; Hannah 68; Jane
  F. 7,8; Jenny 50; Judith 49,65,
  125; Lucy 102; Lydia 41; Mar-
  garet 37; Mary 10,43,44; Maryan
  85,86; Mary Ann 81; Mary
  Frances 97; Nancy 28,109;

Flournoy cont'd.
  Phebe 107,109; Rhoda 38; Sarah
  115; Tabitha 68,111
Folks - Foulkes, Anna 11; Jane 30;
  Mary 100,128; Michal 123; Nancy
  88
Forsee, Elizabeth 97; Judith 55
Fourqueran - Furquren, Martha 89;
  Nancy 54; Polly Ann 90
Fowler, Amasa 15; Elizabeth 1,65;
  Emely 116; Nancy 118; Patsy 14;
  Phebe 119; Sarah 14,99
Franklin-Frankling-Franklyn, Amey
  130; Ann 71; Betsy 36; Elizabeth
  61; Martha 127; Nancy 67,123;
  Polly 2,24; Sally 42
French, Dolly 111
Friend, Ann 78,92,131; Judith 130;
  Martha 36; Mary 36
Frith - Frifty, Rebecca 99; Sally
  33
Fuqua, Elizabeth 69; Mary 88

Gardner, Patsey 108; Rachel G. 27
Garrott, Elizabeth 35
Gary, Elizabeth 65
Gates, Elizabeth 96; Dolly 95;
  Jean 117; Judith 8; Lucy 87;
  Martha 3; Page 15; Phebe 6;
  Priscilla 16,113; Susanna 56
Gatts, Susanna 56
Gibbone, Nancy 86
Gibbs, Martha 126; Mary Ann 101;
  Mary 48; Nancy 42; Phebe 81;
  Rebecca 127
Gibson - Gipson, Hannah 38; Martha
  112; Nancy 50,63
Gill, Anne 6; Betty 83; Elizabeth
  56,104; Frances 72; Jency 57;
  Jensey Elliott 41; Jinny 41;
  Mary 12,42,56; Nancy 94,107;
  Patty 92; Polly 104; Retty 22;
  Sally 17,73; Sophia 71; Susanna
  58,96; Wilmoth 42
Glassco, Fanny 57
Godsey, Elizabeth 109; Frances 68;
  Nancy 16; Sarah 113
Goode, Agnes Epps 121; Ann 50;
  Eliza 97; Elizabeth 72,73; Louisa
  Alice 64; Malinda 113; Margaret
  25; Martha 62,107.126; Mary 85,
  112; Nancy 87; Polly 127; Sally
  B. 79; Sarah 119; Susanna 47;
  Tabitha O. 45
Goodwin - Goodwyn, Frances 37(2);
  Nancy 11; Polly 8; Susanna A. 123
Goodrich, Lucy 116
Googer, Elizabeth 21
Gordon, Barbara 77; Elizabeth 44;
  Mary 25,102; Polly 75(2); Sally
  94
Granger, Elizabeth 58; Nany 40;
  Phebe Eanes 55
Grant, Anne 67
Graves, Alice-Alsey 32; Ann 10;
  Ann Field 80; Dolly 11; Eliza-
  beth 1,125; Frances 49; Lucy 13;
  Nancy J. 14; Sally 41; Sarah 94;
  Rebecca 19
Green, Sally 124

Gregory - Grigory, Ann 27; Eliza
46; Elizabeth 23; Margaret 63;
Mary 61; Sally 131
Grizel. Sarah 109
Gross, Elizabeth 41

Hall, Biddy 59; Mary W. 17;
Phebe 3
Hamblin - Hamlin, Hannah 106;
Polly 70; Sally 11
Hancock, Barbara 65; Betsy 48,
96; Edith 69; Elizabeth 2,87;
Hannah 14; Jensey 81; Keziah
65; Milly 61; Nancy 31,73;
Obedience 20,78; Patsy 127;
Phebe 59; Polly 19; Rhoda 36;
Sally 63,120
Handy, Mary 119
Hardiman, Mary 79
Hardin, Nancy 103
Hare, Mary Ann 31; Mary D. 46
Harris, Betsey 75,113; Elizabeth
75; Martha F. 107
Harrison, Catey 89; Martha 31,80
Haskins, Elizabeth 19,118;
Frances 1; Jane 118; Martha
118; Mary 118; Phebe 25;
Susanna 97
Hatchett, Polly 94
Hatcher, Ann 85; Aggy 66; Asenath
103; Elizabeth 23; Martha 23;
Mary Walthall 38; Mary Green
Hooker 116; Milly 6; Obedience
45; Patsey 68; Tabitha 16
Heath, Lavania 100
Hendrick, Sally 8
Heneage, Sally 8
Henry, Judith 58
Hightower, Nancy 39
Hill, Ann 63; Annie 53; Annis
53; Margaret 50; Mary 22,65,
112; Nancy 70; Polly 61; Pris-
cilla 16; Sarah 83,130,132;
Winifred 79
Hix, Elizabeth 103; Judith 22;
Moley 21; Nancy 78; Rebecca
115; Sally 125
Hobbs, Beedy 64; Polly 84;
Sarah 14
Hocks, Mary 53
Hollidge, Ann 23
Holt, Amelia 39; Ann 8; Frances
64
Hopkins, Mary 107
Horner, Amey 116; Ann 54; Betty
53; Catharine 91; Frances 22;
Lucy 3; Martha 27; Prudence
27; Sarah 24; Tabitha 19,92
Horsley, Rebecca 31,32
Hortler, Rhoda 49
Howard, Polly 58
Howell. Mary 56(2)
Howlett, Elizabeth 71; Elizabeth
Hardie 23; Judith 38
Hoy, Anne 52; Susanna 90
Hubbard, Elizabeth 54; Nancy
27,108; Patsey H. 115
Hudson, Eliza C. 61; Mourning
76; Wine 30
Hundley - Hunley, Elizabeth D.
64; Frances 20

Hutcheson, Jean 15

Ironmonger, Nancy 98
Irwin, Elizabeth 52; Martha 57;
Sally 39; Susanna 110

Jackson, Betsy Dance 72; Judith
12; Lucy 18.21; Martha 26; Mary
128; Miranda 124; Sarah 27
James, Elizabeth 8
Jarrett, Elizabeth 131
Jenkins, Martha 12
Jennings, Polly 49
Johnson, Betsey 91; Elizabeth 132;
Lucy 112; Polly 3; Sarah 39;
Sisley 18; Susanna 6
Jones, Anne Elizabeth 72; Charlotte
40; Elizabeth 66,96; Martha R.
72; Rebecca Edwards 74; Sally
80(2); Sarah 99; Susanna 97;
Unity Claiborne 6; Virginia 117

Keen, Tabitha 53
Kelcher, Ann 77
Kelly, Agnes 132; Rhoda 96
Kelton, Polly 88
Kempton, Anne 86
Kendall - Kendel, Frances 48
Keys, Elizabeth 81; Martha 110
Kleinhoff, Sarah 74
Knibb, Catharine 50

Labarreaire, Sally 49
Lacy, Tabitha 37
Lafon, Elizabeth 66
Landrum, Anne Hankins 17; Eliza-
beth 1
Langsdon, Betsy 62
Laprade - Leprade, Hannah 85;
Martha 65,121; Mary 38; Nancy 92
Lee, Agness 75
Leigh, Elizabeth 64
Lepnor, Susanna 23
Lester, Anne 7; Elizabeth 106;
Martha 32; Polly 108; Sarah 104,
128
Lewis, Rebecca 88
Ligon, Jane 41
Lively, Rebecca 53
Lockett, Anne 20; Elizabeth 7,119;
Jane 67; Lonchey 3; Mary 2(2),
8,28; Phebe 22; Polly 115;
Winney 30
Logwood, Ann F. 84; Edith 65
Loofman, Sarah 26
Lookado - Lucadoe, Elizabeth 73;
Patsey 87; Rebecca 48
Loosey, Betsy 97
Lyle, Sally B. 107

McCollican, Margaret 79
McCoy, Elizabeth 43
McFarland, Margaret 17
McGruder, Nancy 117

Manlove, Jenny 9
Mann, Dicey 94; Gilley 78; Lucy 15;
Martha 130; Mary 94; Mary Green
130; Molly 82; Nancy 35; Phebe
86,126; Prudence 34; Sarah 33;
Virginia 111; Winney 111

Male, Mason 85; Sally 110
Markham, Catherine 102; Eliza-
  beth 101; Judith 35,119; Magee
  4; Mary 16
Marsh, Michey 4; Mickey 5
Marshall, Elizabeth G. 83; Mary
  122
Martin, Elizabeth 7; Janey 63;
  Mary H. 69; Nancy 31; Polly
  44,53; Sarah 76; Ursula 81
Mayo, Maryan 3
Michaels, Elizabeth 107
Miles, Martha 34,79; Nancy 81
Miller, Elizabeth 31
Mitchell, Polly 68
Moody, Elizabeth 128; Mene 73;
  Sally 83
Moore, Agness 5; Basha 88; Betsy
  Jackson 129; Dicey 122; Eliza-
  beth 32,120; Fanny 3,14;
  Frances 123; Levina 68; Lucy
  13; Martha 58; Maxea 21; Mica
  14; Nancy 39; Patty 106; Phebe
  94; Polley 59; Sarah 1
More, Susanna 102
Morgan, Ann 123(2); Kitturah 70;
  Lucy 1; Polly 93; Rebecca 29;
  Sarah 75
Morrissett, Betsy 68; Fanney 1;
  Frances 26; Margaret 7;
  Matilda 76; Polly 45; Salley
  34
Morris, Polly 16; Salley 51
Morrison, Sally 1
Moseley, Elizabeth H. 32,77;
  Frances 76; Martha 133; Patty
  104; Sarah 105; Tabitha 28;
  Virginia Ann 58
Moxley, Polly 31; Rhoda 76;
  Sarah 100
Murchie, Margaret 40

Nece, Sarah Antonnette 85
Newby, Anne 10; Anith 90;
  Armenia 69; Dinah 32; Eliza-
  beth 82; Frances 32,90; Martha
  1,46; Mary 54; Obedience 63;
  Rhody 99; Sarah 10,31; Teina
  89; Winifred 61
Newell, Elizabeth 24,38
Nivins, Susanna 66
Noble - Nobles, Clarissa 5;
  Elizabeth 70; Susannah 17
Norrice - Norris, Dyson 10;
  Phebe 110
Nunnally, Betsey 26; Frances
  108; Hanna 122; Jamima 103;
  Martha 49,62; Mary 60,86,100;
  Nancy 47; Patsey 21; Prudence
  87; Sarah 87; Sosha 28; Sus-
  anna 114

Osborne, Betty Epes 19; Eliza-
  beth 83; Martha 116; Mary 83
Otter, Betsey 18
Owen, Sarah 109

P----, Patience 51
Pankey, Elizabeth 63,76,126;
  Sarah 86; Temperance 51
Parmer, Jane 41; Polly 63

Parry, Nancy 18
Partin, Mary Rowlett 22
Patram - Patrum, Anne 56; Edith
  117; Elizabeth 56,99,115; Fanney
  6; Lucy 104; Phebe 52,130;
  Polly 39; Rebecca 103; Sarah 51
Patterson, Ann 53; Frances 58;
  Lucy 130; Sarah 38
Paul - Paull, Jane 81,85; Mary 13;
  Sally 23
Pearce, Elizabeth 64; Rebecca 60
Perdue, Elizabeth 93; Ellinor 61;
  Fanny 123; Fatey 118; Laurana
  121; Nancy 5; Nanny 46,54; Pheby
  100; Prudence 48,49; Susanna 15,
  32
Perkins, Sarah 25
Perkinson - Purkinson, Agnes 82;
  Betsy 94; Cilla 12; Elizabeth
  131; Judith 105,106; Martha 95;
  Mary 4; Mary Davis 95; Mickey 91;
  Milley 90; Patsey 95; Phebe 80;
  Polly 94,115; Priscilla 95
Perry, Elizabeth 72; Rebecca 72
Philips - Phillips, Clara 129;
  Frances 118
Pilkington - Pilkinton, Mary Ann
  46; Mary 18
Pirdee, Saley 128
Platt, Theodosha Wager 26
Pleasant, Elizabeth 2; Sally 2
Pool - Pooll, Susanna 37
Porter, Phebe W. 30
Potter, Sarah 113
Powell, Disey 108; Elizabeth 28;
  Nancy 98; Susanna 75
Pride, Elizabeth B. 109; Priscilla
  128; Sally 33; Susanna 101
Pritchard, Mary 45; Sidnew 108
Puckett, Ann 67; Betsy 39; Eliza-
  beth 51; Frances 46; Mimey 89;
  Sarah 125; Rebecca 128; Rhoda 11
Puller, Nancy 46
Purdie, Nancy 102

Quarles, Charlotte 60; Mary 68

Railey, Ann 14; Elizabeth 23,100
Randolph, Frances 121; Jane 100;
  Lucy 66; Mary 117; Sally 36
Rigsby, Susanna 25
Ro----, Nelly 74
Roberson, Elizabeth 122; Martha 28
Roberts, Ann 79; Barbara 111; Eliza-
  beth 115,129; Rebecca 76
Robertson, Anne 11,35,125; Betsy
  128; Elizabeth 49,54,122; Jane
  50; Jemima 15; Lucy 28; Martha
  59; Martha Field 20; Mary 9;
  Nancy 51; Patience 55; Phebe 7;
  Sally 35,105; Tabitha 45
Robiou, Charlotte 84
Rofret, Sally 10
Ronald, Jane 105; Sarah 86
Roper, Elizabeth 52; Milly 67;
  Nancy 39; Rhody 24; Sally 107;
  Sarah 115
Rose, Elizabeth 88; Susanna 97
Rowlett, Betsey 104; Elizabeth 58,
  126; Fanny 82; Frances 42,127;
  Hannah 114; Larkey 41; Lockey 93;

139

Williamson, Frances 32; Sarah 39
Wilson - Willson, Ann 15,83; Mary
  81,109; Patsy 58; Polly 112;
  Sally 91,96
Winefred, Wilmouth 128
Winfree - Winfrey, Ann 31; Eliza-
  beth 120,127,130; Judith 125:
  Lucy 97; Lucy Hopson 39;
  Martha 16,33; Miney 129; Polly
  17,67; Susanna 77
Womcak, Ann 20; Elizabeth 35;
  Mary 69; Sally 127; Sarah 86,
  111; Susanna 112
Wood, Mary 76; Sarah 112
Woodson, Jane T. 92
Woodcock, Elizabeth 1; Faney 54
Wooldridge, ----- 78; Betsyan
  43; Caroline 34,44; Frances H.
  7; Hannah 44; Martha 125;
  Mary A. 73; Nancy J. 117;
  Permelia B. 34; Sallee 113;
  Sally 128
Worsham, Elizabeth 106; Lucy
  102,104; Martha 42,60,114;
  Mary 67,93; Nancy 67; Rebecca
  10,60; Sarah 10
Wray, Mary 92,126
Wright, Tabitha 101
Wyatt - Wiatt, Elizabeth 110;
  Lavinia 94

Young, Dorothy 62